GOD'S Love Song

*To Barb —
God Bless you!
Jenny Allen*

God's Love
Song

GINNY ALLEN

Pacific Press®
Publishing Association

Nampa, Idaho | Oshawa, Ontario, Canada
www.pacificpress.com

Edited by Penny Estes Wheeler
Cover design by Gerald Lee Monks
Cover illustration by iStockphoto.com
Inside design by Kristin Hansen-Mellish

Library of Congress Cataloging-in-Publication Data:

Allen, Ginny.
 God's love song / Ginny Allen
  p. cm.
 ISBN 13: 978-0-8163-3902-0 (pbk.)
 ISBN 10: 0-8163-3902-3 (pbk.)
 1. Allen, Ginny. 2. Seventh-day Adventists—United States—Biography I. Title.
 BX6193.A385A3 2012
 286.7092—dc23
 [B]

                              2012026341

 13 14 15 16   •   5 4 3 2

If tears could be caught and set
like diamonds in a coronet,
would we set their price exceedingly small
because they are so common to us all,
or would we count each one
a priceless gem
because of the pain producing them?

—Ginny Allen

This book is dedicated to my family for their loving support in everything I do!

My husband David—first my friend and then my eternal love. He has always encouraged me in whatever I do, but especially and most importantly, in my walk with God.
He has long wanted to see my stories in print, so this is for him.

My son Scott has given me joy since the moment I first held him. He is everything a son should be. He has blessed my life with his love.

My daughters-in-law, Cathie and Dana, are the daughters my heart always longed for. I could not have chosen better. Thank you to my sons for this gift.

My grandchildren, Ashley and Kennedy, are the sunshine in my heart. Every moment with them is treasured. They give me sweet contentment as I watch them grow into women of God.

And in sweet memory of my son Bob who left us too soon. We look forward to reunion on Resurrection Day.

And a special thank you to Penny Estes Wheeler, my editor and favorite author since she first began to write. Her thoughts are exquisite, and her writing is superb.

Contents

Introduction   9

In That Moment   11

Intrusion   15

Terror in the Night   19

Always Afraid   23

Breaking Hearts   27

Beginning Again   31

Introduced to Jesus   35

A Changed Life   41

God Plans My Life   45

Life Is Good   51

Things Don't Matter   57

Bad News   61

The Worst   67

The Longest Night   73

God Understands   77

Bad News Again   83

God Knows   89

Promises   95

From Bad to Worse   103

No Untouchables   109

Free Wash   115

Epilogue: Blessed, So Very Blessed   121

Introduction

My prayer, as you read this book—written just for you—is that you will see a picture of a God who loves you so much He can't imagine eternity without you.

The stories are from my journey with God. Even in my childhood, at a time I didn't know Him, He knew me. And He loved me more than I could ever imagine, the very same way He loves you.

The Bible promises I have chosen to share are meant to remind you that we have a God who rejoices over us with singing. I like to think that these special promises are God's love song for each one of us. Hold them to your heart as you read them. Know that each promise comes directly from God and is just for you. God's promises are the most important part of this book.

"The LORD your God in your midst, the Mighty One, will save; He will rejoice over you with gladness, He will quiet you in His love, He will rejoice over you with singing" (Zephaniah 3:17, NKJV).

Chapter 1

In That Moment

On a warm Friday afternoon in the late summer of 1971, my doorbell rang, and my life changed again.

We had just moved to Laurelwood Academy, a Seventh-day Adventist Christian high school in the hills outside of Portland, Oregon. My husband was going to be teaching religion there as part of the curriculum. I thought the doorbell had probably been rung by one of the neighborhood children coming to play with our boys, who were four and five years old. Instead, I found myself facing a dark-eyed stranger.

I opened the screen door a polite distance and said, "Hello! What can I do for you?"

With a wistful smile, the man asked, "Don't you know who I am?"

I studied him for a moment. He was short, stocky, middle-aged, and wearing a worn tan shirt.

"No, I'm sorry," I said. "I don't. Is there something I can do for you?" But even as the words left my mouth, I felt the first flicker of recognition.

"You really don't know?" he queried with a small, sad smile.

Suddenly I did know, but from deep inside there came a refusal to admit the truth.

"I'm your father."

In that moment, I was four years old again. I was standing by the couch where my mother had fallen when my father—this man—had struck her. And I heard my small voice begging, "Please wake up, Mommy! Please, please, wake up!"

In that moment, I was a little girl fleeing from home late at night with my mother and my sister, a mere eighteen months older than I was. With us were the few possessions we could carry in our small suitcases, and we huddled alone on the dark, deserted platform, waiting for the train that would take us to safety, the train that would take us away from my father.

In that moment, I was a small eight-year-old girl cowering in a bedroom in the wee hours of the morning. Beyond the thin door, the house trembled with the force and sound of plates shattering on the kitchen walls as a deep voice screamed in drunkenness and a higher voice shouted in anger.

In that moment, I was a teenager and secretly glad that my father was not coming to my graduation because how could I ever explain him to my friends? I was a Christian now, graduating from a Christian high school, and felt certain that no one there would understand that my father was an alcoholic.

On that warm September afternoon, the stranger said, "I'm your father," and in that moment I wished, oh, how I wished, that he were not my father.

And that he would turn and go away.

"I knew you before I formed you in your mother's womb"
(Jeremiah 1:5, NLT).

I am not alone.

There are too many similar moments in too many lives, moments that many women, like myself, would like to erase from their memories. But the good news is that God knows about those moments, and He promises that He still has a plan for your life. His Word says it plainly: " 'I know the plans I have for you,' declares the LORD, 'plans to prosper you and not to harm you, plans to give you hope and a future' " (Jeremiah 29:11).

Someone has said, "Your past does not determine your future." There is so much truth in that simple sentence. We do not have to let what has happened to us in the past determine what we will be in the future. The good news is that no matter what has happened in your life, no matter what your beginnings might have been, God sees you as His loved-beyond-words child.

I have two grandchildren, and I think they are the most beautiful girls in the entire world. When I say they are beautiful, I am not talking about how they look. Of course I think that Ashley with her red hair and green eyes and Kennedy with blond hair and similar green eyes are gorgeous, but that is not what makes them beautiful.

I thought they were beautiful the moment I first held them. Back when they were just moments old and had not yet smiled or said funny things or walked on wobbly legs to come to me, I declared each one beautiful. They were still a little wrinkly and red, with yet unfocused eyes when I whispered my love, "You are so beautiful!" Those few words bring together everything I feel about them—the joy, the wonder, the hope. The happiness that floods my heart at the mere thought of each of my girls is beyond my ability to express. They make my heart sing as no one else can do.

The wonder is that God feels the same way about you. He declared His love for you long before you smiled at Him or prayed to Him or took your first steps leading to Him. You make His heart sing. His words in Zephaniah 3:17 are meant for you.

"The LORD your God is with you; his power gives you victory. The LORD will take delight in you, and in his love he will give you new life. He will sing and be joyful over you" (TEV).

What a picture! God joyfully singing His love over each one of us! I remember the first time I read that verse. I quickly went to my prayer journal and turned to the list of questions I want to someday ask God. My questions are not deep, nor are they theological. Not one of them is big or heavy. They are just things I wonder about, things I want to know.

One of the questions is about birds. I wrote it down. "God, do all birds sound good when they sing? I don't mean the difference between a crow and a canary. But if you put two canaries side by side and let them sing, do the other canaries say, 'Wow, that one is really good, but this other one ought to keep its beak shut'?"

Another question is about cats. "God, how do cats purr?"

Scientists understand very little about the purr mechanism in cats. They know approximately where it comes from and a little of how it operates, but purring is still somewhat of a scientific mystery. I love to feel their engines start at the first touch of my hand on soft kitty fur. God put the purr in the pussycat (and the lion and the tiger), so I know that someday He can explain it to me.

I had another question the first time I read Zephaniah 3:17.

I went straight to my list of questions and wrote, "Dear God, what is the song You are singing over me? Did You make it up just for me? Does it have my name in it? Is it the same song each time You sing for me, or sometimes is it different?

"I hope it's a happy song because I try so hard to bring You joy! I want to live so that You will rejoice over me with singing."

I continued, "God, someday when I am in heaven, can we go for a walk together and will You sing for me the song You sing over me now? And when You do, in some deep part of my soul, will I recognize my song because You are so much a part of my life?"

I think God has a song for each one of us. I don't think He has just one song that covers us all, but rather that He has a unique song for each one of us. Maybe we each have our own unique love songs from God. In my imagination, I picture God in heaven singing His song over me, and the angels hear it. I imagine them saying to each other, "God is singing again. Listen, He's singing Ginny's song!" Or He's singing your song. Maybe right now, at this moment, God is singing *your* song. Can you hear it deep in your heart?

Chapter 2

Intrusion

It had been almost twenty years since I'd last seen my father. I was eleven years old at the time. Since then I had received few letters from him. An occasional Christmas or birthday card came with a few lines scrawled at the bottom. That was all.

Now here he stood, just inches away, an intrusion on the life I had built without him.

I must have said all the right things—"Won't you come in? Can you stay for supper?"—because soon he and his wife, who had been waiting in the car, were sitting in my sunny living room.

How can you not have a single thing to say to your own father?

I should have had a million things I wanted to tell him. But I, who can talk to absolutely anyone, could not think of anything to say, not even polite first-time-company conversation.

I should have gone to the door and called our two boys in from playing. After all, they were his grandsons. But how could I explain who this man was? He had nothing to do with my life, or with theirs. They must have sensed my feelings when they came in later, because from the kitchen I heard my four-year-old in the living room trying to sort out the relationship. He was asking in a puzzled voice, "Wanna see my truck? Uncle? Mister?"

I took both boys aside and explained who this man was in terms that they could understand. Up until then they didn't even know he existed. I told them to call this man who was really their grandfather whatever felt comfortable to them. The boys chose to call him "Uncle."

You see, Grandpa was not this dark-eyed stranger. Their grandpa was back in Missouri in the house by the creek. That was all right. I didn't want to hear them call this man "Grandpa." In fact, I was having a similar conflict. My mind kept saying, *This man is your father.* But my heart argued back, *No, he isn't! My dad is back in Missouri in the house by the creek.*

This man, this stranger now sitting on my living room couch, had walked out of my life when I was only four years old. He was nothing to me now.

"I will not fail you or abandon you"
(Joshua 1:5, NLT).

To be abandoned is to feel unloved. The feeling of being abandoned is one of the most devastating emotions we can experience. And to be rescued gives the exact opposite feeling. The sense of relief, the thankfulness, the utter joy at being rescued! There is no way to adequately express this in words.

I know both—being abandoned and being rescued.

I like being rescued better.

I remember standing on the banks of the Snake River when I was a little girl. As I watched people in large rafts floating down the river, I dreamed that someday I would do that too. It didn't happen for me until much later in my life. But finally the day came.

My husband, Dave, was a Bible teacher, and I was the school nurse at Auburn Adventist Academy near Seattle. One year the school staff decided that we and our families would take a summer float trip down the Snake in Idaho.

I was excited but a little afraid as I put on one of the large orange Mae West life jackets that Drury's Drifters required each of us to wear. I made sure that I was sitting on the side of the large raft where I could hold on to the attached rope that encircles the entire raft. That rope felt like my safety line. Our two boys sat just in front of me, at the very front of the raft. Dave chose to do the trip in a small two-person inflatable kayak.

For the first few hours, everything went well. We easily rode one stretch of rapids after another, and I began to relax. Finally, I decided that I could let go of the rope, my safety line, and enjoy the ride. Just then we went around a bend in the river and plunged into the roughest, wildest rapids we experienced on the entire trip.

As we hit the first violent whitewater, the raft stood up vertically on the long side—and that's how it went through the entire stretch of rapids. Dr. Drury later said he never saw a raft stand up so straight without flipping over. And in the instant that the raft stood up, I was washed right over the lower side along with my younger son Bob. Both of us grabbed hold of the rope along the side, and that is how we went through the entire stretch of rapids.

As we were being pulled and jerked through the violent rapids, waves trying to drown us and rocks challenging our survival, thoughts raced through my desperate mind. *If I let go of the rope, I'll be sucked under the water and I'll drown. If that doesn't happen, then I'd surely hit my head on a rock, be knocked unconscious, and drown. And if that didn't happen, then the rafts will race on ahead of me and leave me behind. I'll have to walk out of the canyon alone, but I can't possibly do that and survive!*

These frightening thoughts flew through my mind far more quickly then I can tell them. And all the while my friends in the raft were shouting, "Hang on, Ginny! Hang on!"

Why do they think I would let go? I thought desperately. The rest of my life depended on my hanging on to that rope.

It was about then that I realized my twelve-year-old son had his arm around me while he clung to the rope with his other hand. He was saying over and over to me, "You're OK, Mom. I have you. I'm holding you. I won't let you go."

The feeling of knowing you are safe is indescribable. The moment of rescue brings sweet relief that soars far beyond the simple meaning of that word. God understands that sometimes in our lives we need rescue. Isaiah 43:1–5 is God's promise of rescue. This promise is for you.

> Don't be afraid. I have rescued you. I have called you by name; now you belong to me. When you cross deep rivers, I will be with you, and you won't drown. When you walk through fire, you won't be burned or scorched by the flames. I am the Lord, your God, the Holy One of Israel, the God who saves you. . . . To me, you are very dear, and I love you. That's why I gave up nations and people to rescue you. Don't be afraid! I am with you (CEV).

Everywhere I go I find people who feel as if they have fallen out of life's raft. They feel as if they are going to drown in their own tears. Or that they must walk through the fires in their lives alone, and they can't do that and survive. But also, everywhere I go, there are encouraging voices shouting, "Hang on! Hang on!" There are people who are promising, "I have you. I'm holding you. I won't let you go."

God is the One who rescues us, but He also uses people in our lives to encourage us through the tough times. He uses your voice and my voice. He uses your hands and my hands. He uses us to be "God with skin on." And once you have been rescued, you can never stand idly by while others drown.

God wants to use you. But first He wants to rescue you, if that's what you need right now. Maybe He's whispering in your ear, "I have you. I'm holding you. I won't let you go."

Chapter 3

Terror in the Night

Yes, I had a few memories of my father, but they weren't the kind you put in a memory book. I suppose I was too young when we left him for me to remember much. I was only four years old when the marriage ended. Too young to think that it had anything to do with me.

My father had been away in the navy during World War II, and when he came home to Bremerton, Washington, he never really came home. He had become an alcoholic, and now he spent most of his free time drinking in local bars.

I have few memories of those days. We had a big dog named Blackie, who sat patiently while my sis and I dressed her in our clothes. There was a babysitter whom we called Big Phyl so we wouldn't confuse her with my sister who was also named Phyllis. I can look back and clearly see the pink roses climbing the trellis on the porch of our little white house. I think the reason I remember those roses so clearly is that they were the only things of beauty in my life.

I don't remember any play times. I don't remember Daddy tucking his little girls into bed for the night. But I remember the night when, in his drunkenness, he hit my mother and knocked her out. And I remember the night when we finally left, just the three of us with our three small suitcases.

Through the years, I wondered why there were so few mementos of my childhood. My mother-in-law had saved everything of my husband's growing-up years—his first shoes, his tiny silver baby spoon, his trucks and his train, his first teddy bear, and a much loved pink elephant. She saved every coloring book and later most of his school workbooks. And carefully stored in the attic were pictures of every important event and many not-so-important events. My heart questioned, *Why hadn't my mother saved* my *things? Weren't they important to her?*

From my young life nothing was saved except a few pictures and my World War II ration book. So little to show of the little girl I was then.

Then suddenly I remembered the three small suitcases. There was no room in them for anything that wasn't vital to our lives.

I remember that frightening night as we waited for the train to arrive. We stood outside on the train platform, and I remember trying to find shadows to hide in, in case my father came and found us before we could get away. Most of all I remember the fear—the heart-pounding terror of that night—and the questions that had no answers. *What if he comes after us? What if he finds us? Will he hit my mother again? What if something happens to her? Who will take care of us then?*

"The Lord your God goes with you;
he will never leave you nor forsake you"
(Deuteronomy 31:6).

I wish I'd known then what I know now.

I wish someone had told me about the God who loves me and who promises, "I will never leave you nor forsake you." I wish I had known the God who promises, "I'm holding you by your right hand."

But I didn't know Him, and there seemed to be no one in my life to tell me. But I am no longer the little girl who didn't know. When I found the God who had walked through life with me, holding me when I didn't know I was being held, my life changed forever. So I am determined that as people walk in and out of my life, they will meet the God who can change their lives. Let none be able to say, "There was no one to tell me."

I met Kallie during my first year as a school nurse in an inner-city high school. She told me her story. She was a prostitute at the age of ten. She had her first baby when she was just barely twelve years old. That baby was taken from her to live with relatives in the South, and Kallie never saw her again. She was pregnant again at the age of fourteen, and gave birth to a little girl who died before she was a year old. There was a question of neglect in the death because of the circumstances involved— an all-night card party with drinking and drugs and a crying baby whose last cries were never answered.

When I met Kallie, she was in the last of a series of foster homes. In the two years that I knew her, she was frequently on probation—for being a runaway, for arson, for petty theft, for breaking curfew, for prostitution, for drugs, and more. Her dad was serving a life sentence in prison.

Her mom's new boyfriend moved in just after Kallie's sixth birthday. Mom's boyfriend didn't like children, and so Mom had to make a choice.

One day when Kallie came home from school, Mom told her that she, Kallie, had to leave. Mom said that she could not live there anymore.

So Kallie simply moved out and lived on the streets. She was six years old and in the first grade. What does a six-year-old know about how to take care of herself!

I asked her, "Kallie, how did you live?"

"I ate out of garbage cans," she said, "and slept under bridges."

Her story was so unbelievable that I asked her social worker if it was true. She said that everything Kallie had told me was true, and then added, "But it's much worse than what she has told you."

Kallie used to come in frequently to talk to me, sometimes two or three times a day. Often she would stand behind my chair and slip her fingers through the curls at the back of my neck. She just wanted to talk. She just wanted someone to be interested in her. Kallie was never special to anyone. She never had that special someone whose eyes could tell her that she was worth something, that she was valuable, that she was loved.

All Kallie had was a mirror, and a mirror wasn't enough to show her value.

A court date was set for the arson charge. Kallie had tried to burn down a local Lutheran school. She knew she would be found guilty and would have to go to the detention center unit until she was twenty-one.

I promised her that I would go with her to the hearing. I told her, "Kallie, I can't change the sentence, but I will go with you and be with you no matter what."

But perhaps for the first time in her life, Kallie was afraid. She ran away that next September, and we never saw her or heard from her again.

I used to look for her as I drove through the streets of the city. One day I asked a policeman assigned to our school if he had ever seen her after she had disappeared. He said that he hadn't, and then added, "Kallie is exactly the kind of girl that we will find dead under a bridge someday. There's no one to look out for her. There's no one in her life who cares if she's dead or alive."

But even though we never saw her again, God has never lost sight of Kallie. Even when we don't see the end of the story, God is still involved in the story. He does not walk away when the details aren't pretty to look at. He means it when He says in Deuteronomy 31:8, "The LORD himself will lead you and be with you. He will not fail you or abandon you, so do not lose courage or be afraid" (TEV).

I hope that as long as she lives, Kallie will remember that there was a school nurse who loved her. I hope she will remember that there was a nurse who listened to her and did not turn away from her touch. I hope Kallie will think of the Bible promises I shared and remember that none of us are truly alone. Oh, how I hope that Kallie will remember that she is God's girl and He is walking beside her no matter what has happened in her life.

Those promises are for you too. God is involved in your story. Even when you don't see the end, God never loses sight of you. So don't lose courage, and don't be afraid.

Chapter 4

Always Afraid

The long train ride from Bremerton, Washington, ended in Denver, Colorado, where we lived with my grandparents for several years. At the end of my second-grade year at Sacred Heart Elementary School, my mother started dating a man named Clem.

I don't remember much about him except that I was afraid of him. My sister and I didn't like to be around him. We would shrink against the wall, holding on to each other whenever he came near us. My mother quickly realized that he was not only not what she wanted, but he was not even what he said he was! But when she tried to end the relationship, he threatened her, telling her what would happen if she tried to leave him. And so we found ourselves running away again, just the three of us. This time we went to Seattle to be near an aunt and uncle who could help us.

It was about six months later that Clem found us. One day when I was at school, my third-grade teacher received a phone call saying that my sister and I could not be released to anyone except the police, no matter who the person claimed to be.

My classroom was on the front side of the building, so I was excited to see a police car pull up to the school. But moments later, the excitement turned to fear when I and my sister were led to the police car. The police officers took us to my aunt's house. We all went inside and my sister and I listened through a crack at the bedroom door as the police explained the situation to my aunt.

Clem had found us. He had called my mother at her job and said that if she wouldn't cooperate with him, he would "get her girls." He gave the name of the school we attended and told Mother that he would be waiting for us there. He talked about throwing acid on us if he could get close enough. Then he said there were other things he could do to us too, but my heart stopped when I heard about the acid. I don't think I need to tell you what that kind of fear does to the heart of an eight-year-old child.

Late that night my sister and I, just eight and nine years old, were sent alone on a ferry across Puget Sound to Bremerton to stay with my father and his wife, Doris, so we would be safe. Clem didn't know who my father was, so he would not be able to find us there. It seemed to me that the hour-long ferry ride took forever, yet in another terrible way it was over in seconds!

Four years before I had trembled with fear when a train took us away in the night, away from my father. And now my small body trembled with fear again as the ferry carried us away in the darkness, away from Clem, but back to a man I barely recognized. Back to the father I hadn't seen since we fled from him four years before.

"I am the Lord, your God, who takes hold of your right hand and says to you, Do not fear; I will help you"
(Isaiah 41:13).

I almost never think of Clem, except to wonder what may have happened to him later in his life. I don't like to think that he continued through life exactly as he was when I knew him. So when I think of him, I pray that he found the God who can change lives. I pray that he let God change him.

I have always loved animals. Anything with fur makes me purr like a kitten. And speaking of kittens reminds me of our sweet Chum, a huge Siamese cat that owned us for almost fourteen years.

When Chum died, four people cried—I cried, and so did my husband and our two sons. It's not that he was such a good cat, and certainly he wasn't worth much money, even though he was Siamese. But he was our cat and we loved him. And Chum was a lover. If you came to our house and sat down, he would instantly be on your lap. He would put his front paws around your neck and snuggle in as if he'd known you forever. He just assumed you would love him too.

But I am the first one to admit that Chum had a few character problems. For one thing, he loved to fight. He fought so often and so hard that his ears were ragged around the edges. In fact, it looked as if they had been trimmed with pinking shears. And one memorable day he came home from a fight with a broken, bloody nose. After that, he couldn't purr. When he tried to purr, he just kind of snorted through his nose.

His other big problem was that he loved baked goods. He could never resist them. That meant that he tried every loaf of bread in the house before we ever got to it. He sampled his way through breads and pies and cakes and cupcakes. He would wait until the cupcakes were cooling on the counter, then make a mad dash through the kitchen, jump on the countertop, and grab a cupcake. Cupcake in mouth, he would run wildly into my bedroom and dive under the bed, stopping right under the center of the bed to eat his stolen treat. He knew my arms weren't long enough to reach him there.

One day when I was making homemade pizza, Chum smelled the crust prebaking. Chum watched as I took the pizza crust from the oven and carefully spread pizza sauce all the way to its edge. When I turned to get the rest of the toppings, Chum made one huge leap onto the countertop to check it out—landing right in the middle of the pizza!

He didn't like the sauce on his feet, and I didn't like his feet on the sauce! He leaped down as quickly as he'd leaped up there and took off. It took me a long time to wipe up all the orange footprints left behind as he ran through the house.

The time I made twelve pumpkin pies for a Thanksgiving party for my son's class I warned everyone in the family to make sure Chum stayed outside. But he smelled the pies and somehow sneaked in the door. About a half hour before the party, I discovered that he'd taken one bite out of the center of each pie. We were expecting 100 kids in thirty minutes. So I did the same thing you would do. I simply cut out the cat-bite part and filled the hole with whipped cream. No one knew the difference except Chum and me.

I have to admit to you that many things Chum did made me unhappy. In fact, many of my friends used to say, "Ginny, how can you put up with that cat? He is a thief, and he can't even purr right."

But I always told them that he was my cat, and I loved him no matter what. And when he died, I cried for that old scruffy, ragged-ear, thieving cat. I always wished he would behave better, but I loved him no matter what. And he knew it.

When I think of Chum, it encourages me in my relationship with God. If I could love an old, troublesome cat so much, then how must God feel about me? I'm sure there are many things He wishes I would do differently because I, too, have a few character problems. But God loves me, utterly and completely, just the way I am, no matter what.

Romans 5:8 confirms how He feels about me and, yes, you too. "God demonstrates his own love toward us in this: While we were still sinners, Christ died for us."

That verse encourages me so much because that's good news! God loves you and me utterly and completely, just the way we are, no matter what. But I'm also glad that He loves us too much to leave us the way we are. And not only does God love those who love Him back, He loves people like Clem, people who hurt us as Clem hurt me. I know that as hurtful people like Clem journey through life, there are things God wishes they would do differently. But He loves them still, utterly and completely.

And that's good news too.

Chapter 5

Breaking Hearts

Now that Phyllis and I were back with our dad, I wish I could tell you that everything was finally all right. But it wasn't.

My most distinct memory of that time is listening in the dark for the footsteps that would tell us they had finally come home. Every evening my father would go to the local taverns and bars for a night of drinking. Bremerton was a navy town, and there were plenty of places to keep him busy. And every evening after we were in bed, my tall, blond stepmother, Doris, who we had just met for the first time, would go out into the night to find him.

My sister and I would huddle close together in bed. We were afraid to be alone, yet afraid for them to come home. We never talked. We just listened for their footsteps, the footsteps that would tell us they were back, for Doris went from bar to bar until she found him. Sometimes it was right away but other nights it took her hours. When she found him, she would drag him home, sometimes by the hair.

When at last we heard them come in, we pretended to be asleep, lying rigid and dreading the fight that always followed. I hated the yelling and screaming that was always punctuated with plates shattering against the kitchen walls. In the morning the food-streaked walls wouldn't let us forget what we had pretended not to hear.

When I look back on it now, I know that Doris was a good woman even though she never tried to be a mother to us. I know now that she was too busy trying to hold her marriage together. She was too busy to worry about two little girls who missed their mother, two little girls who were afraid of their father, two little girls who still feared that Clem would find them.

She was too busy to worry about two little girls whose hearts were breaking.

"No, I will not abandon you or leave you as orphans in the storm — I will come to you"
(John 14:18, TLB).

I understand breaking hearts. My childhood experiences left me with an understanding gained only by living through it. But those experiences have not been wasted, for God has used my understanding to help those who are broken by the events of their lives.

For most of my nursing career, I have been a school nurse. One day when I was working at an elementary school, I found a note from the nurse who had worked there the day before. It asked me to call a parent whose daughter had been excluded from school because she had head lice. Of course, parents often are not happy when they're called to come to the school to pick up their child because of lice. Sometimes they have to leave work, or else they must find someone else to come get their child. Then the child has to stay home until the treatment for lice has been done. So I was supposed to call this mom and ask her if she had treated her daughter yet.

The nurse's note also said that the mom was very angry and would probably be very hostile. So I was not looking forward to making this call. In fact, I put it off as long as I could. Finally, I made myself pick up the phone. The other nurse was right. When the mother answered the phone and I told her who I was and what I wanted, she was, indeed, very hostile.

She started swearing at me and never stopped for almost twenty minutes. She could talk faster than I could think. And I can talk very fast.

While she was screaming obscenities at me, I said to myself, *Ginny, you don't have to take this. You are a professional. Just tell her that you are going to hang up, and that you will be glad to talk to her when she calms down.* But then God gave me one of those little nudges He often gives His children. The thought came clearly—*Just listen to her, Ginny. Just be quiet and let her talk.*

It wasn't easy. But I let her talk. I knew that everyone has to take a breath sometime, so after what seemed like forever she paused for a second, and I jumped into the conversation.

"It sounds like there's more than head lice going on in your life," I said softly.

There was silence on the other end of the line; then she began to cry. Finally, she almost whispered, "You're right. There is."

I asked her gently, "Would you like to tell me about it?"

She began to talk again, this time softly and slowly. She told me that the "head lice thing" was just the last straw. She said that her husband was on death row and was scheduled to be executed in two days. He would die on Thursday night. Today was Tuesday.

"How do you tell your eight-year-old daughter that her daddy is being put to death?" she asked, punctuating her words with soft sobbing. "He did what they said he did, but how do you tell your child?"

Then she told me that her house was being repossessed because she couldn't pay the taxes, so she was being evicted on Friday, the day after her husband's execution. She said they would have to live in her car, which was not running, and she didn't have money for gas even if it were running.

"After Friday," she whispered in a broken voice, "I don't even know how I am going to feed my daughter."

She was sobbing audibly through this whole thing and finally she whispered, "Nurse Ginny, I keep asking God, 'How am I going to get through this?' "

I gave her suggestions of agencies that could help her and told her how to access them. Then we just talked about God. We talked about how He never leaves us no matter how it seems. I shared with her the verses that tell how He walks through life with us. I cried with her and prayed with her. We talked for a long time.

When we finally finished talking, she said, "Ginny, I feel that you are an angel God sent to help me."

———•◦•———

It is both incredible and humbling that God can use us to bring hope to a hurting heart. All of those bad and sad experiences that we wish had never happened to us give us an understanding that we might not otherwise have. Of course, we still wish for idyllic lives—which is God's ultimate plan for us. That's what heaven is all about.

The promises in Revelation show God's plan for His children. "God's home is now with his people. He will live with them, and they will be his own. Yes, God will make his home among his people. He will wipe all tears from their eyes, and there will be no more death, suffering, crying, or pain. These things of the past are gone forever" (Revelation 21:3, 4, CEV).

But until then, we can allow God to use our experiences to make a healing difference in the life of someone whose heart is breaking.

I understand breaking hearts. But I also understand mended hearts. You see, I have one.

Chapter 6

Beginning Again

Now I need to backtrack just a little. It was just a few months before Clem discovered where we were living that my mother met the man she later married, the man who became my stepdad. His name was Bob, and he was the one who sent us to safety that night and followed through with police protection. We never saw nor heard of Clem again, and my mother and Bob were married the following February.

When school ended that late spring, my sister and I went to live with our mother and new stepfather. This man became not just my stepfather but the only real dad I had ever had. It was this dad who introduced me to Jesus. This is the man I mean when I refer to "my dad." I am an example of one of the success stories of stepparenting.

This was the first really happy time in my life. It was truly a new beginning. If you saw pictures of me as a little girl, you would find that I am almost never smiling. When I think back to those years, I never see myself as a happy, carefree child. Life was painful. But now with our new dad, our lives became happy at last.

Well, happy except for the one weekend every month that my sister and I were required by law to spend with our father in Bremerton. Every single month it was the same. Our parents would put us on the ferry in Seattle. All the way across the Sound I would pretend that I was going someplace else. I couldn't allow myself to think of what it would be like when we got to Bremerton. And I always hoped we would be on the Kalakala Ferry with its silver streamlined shape. For some reason, that particular ferry helped me forget what was ahead.

My father and his wife would be waiting for us, and they were always full of hugs and kisses. I let myself be hugged and kissed and tried not to think that the weekend was just starting. Nothing had changed, not the drinking nor the fighting. The food-streaked walls were a constant reminder of violent words and explosive tempers. In the mornings my sister and I were still pretending.

Even with my sister by my side, I felt lost and alone. How could three days last forever?

"He gathers the lambs in his arms
and carries them close to his heart"
(Isaiah 40:11).

I have heard it said that time is relative. I guess that means that how you feel about time relates to what you are doing or what is happening to you. Moments can seem like eternity and hours can seem like seconds. That seems especially true when you are lost or alone or lost *and* alone.

———

We moved to Laurelwood Academy in the summer of 1971, and that first night we unpacked enough to be able to sleep in our own beds. Sometime in the middle of the night, I woke up and heard a child crying. The sound came from outside. I hadn't yet met any of our neighbors, but in my sleep-fogged mind, I assumed one of them must have a small child. I was exhausted from travel and all the unpacking so quickly fell back asleep.

I woke up a little later to hear the same crying. This time I sat up and listened with more concern. It sounded familiar. Too familiar. I got up and ran down the hall toward the front door, glancing into the boys' bedroom as I went. The empty bottom bunk confirmed what my heart already knew. My little boy, just four and a half years old, was crying outside our front door.

Now the words came clearly. "Mommy, please let me in! Mommy, Mommy, I'm so cold! Please let me in!"

When I opened the door, he fell into my arms, sobbing as if his heart were broken. I tucked him into bed between my husband and me, holding him close until his little body warmed up and he fell into a deep sleep.

The next morning he explained that he got up to go to the bathroom and somehow found himself outside with the door locked. I realized that when he got up he made all the turns for the home we had just left in California, which meant he ended up on the front porch in this new house. The door had locked automatically behind him. I don't think I need to tell you how I felt when I realized that my baby had been locked outside, cold and crying for help that was too long in coming. It must have seemed like forever to him.

He cuddled into my arms in sweet relief when the door was opened. He was no longer lost. He was not alone. The warmth of my arms told him what he needed to know. He was safe.

The Bible reminds us in Isaiah 49:15, 16 that Jesus is our safe place. "The Lord says, 'Can a woman forget her baby? Can she forget the child who came from her body? Even if she can forget her children, I cannot forget you. I drew a picture of you on my hand. You are always before my eyes' " (ERV).

This same God who loves us so much He cannot forget us—whose love is so deep that He wrote our names on His hand—this same God wants us to know that even when we feel lost, He is there. He wants us to remember that when we feel totally alone, He is still there. How many times does He tell us in His Word that He will never leave us? Perhaps He said it so many times because He knew we needed to hear it often.

And when we are safe with Him, it's good to open the door and welcome the lost and the lonely into the warmth. God's arms are big enough to hold us all.

Chapter 7

Introduced to Jesus

Three years later, when I was in the sixth grade, my father inexplicably sued for custody of my sister and me. I remember trying to answer seemingly endless questionings put to us by the lawyers. How could you ever say what you really thought when you knew with absolute certainty that your answers would be repeated and you might have to live with someone who might not like what you had said? And anyway, you can't bear the thought of any more heartache or pain. I can't explain the insanity of those days. Again, it seemed a forever time.

Still, I know that I was one of the lucky ones. I was never hit or abused either physically or sexually. It was only my heart that was hurt. But I was left with a lifelong sensitivity to harsh words and raised voices.

My mom and stepdad were finally granted permanent custody of us. The monthly visits to my father would continue. But when the court battle was over, my mom and stepdad took the two of us girls and moved far away to the Midwest.

After we moved, my father never came to see me. He never sent the money for us to come see him, nor did he ever send custody support. He didn't come for my graduation. He didn't come for my wedding. He seldom wrote.

But it was a relief when I didn't have to make the required visits. Maybe it was a relief, too, that he didn't come see us or send for us, his two little girls. I had grown to love my stepdad very much, and he became the only dad my heart acknowledged.

It was this father who taught me to laugh. It was this father who encouraged me to let my sanguine personality shine through. It was this father, this dad, who taught me to believe in myself, to know that I could do anything that I really wanted to do! It was this dad who saw me off on my first date, who puffed up proudly at my school programs, and exclaimed over report cards. It was this dad who walked me down the aisle on my wedding day. He was the one for whom our younger son was named.

It was this dad who introduced me to Jesus.

"Yes, God loved the world so much that he gave his only Son, so that everyone who believes in him would not be lost but have eternal life"
(John 3:16, ERV).

I like meeting new people. I listen carefully during the introductions so I will remember their names. Still, sometimes I forget who they are. But when I was introduced to Jesus, my life was changed forever. You can't forget someone who changes your life that much. You remember not just their name but everything about them. All the little details are engraved in your mind. So it is with Jesus. He took a young girl and transformed her life. How could I ever forget what He did for me?

One Friday afternoon I was cleaning my house when I heard a terrible commotion in the front yard. I ran out just in time to see two large crows drop something in the road by the curb. Close behind the crows, two robins were circling and crying.

I didn't know much about the habits of crows, so I didn't understand what was happening.

As I turned to go back into the house, I saw a pickup truck coming down the street.

As the driver neared our house, he swerved to scare the crows away, for they had continued to dive-bomb whatever it was they had dropped in the road. By then I was curious, so I ran out there to see what was really going on.

There in the gutter lay a baby robin. The crows had stolen him from his nest. His face was bleeding where they had pecked out one eye. His rump was raw near the tail where they had attacked again and again.

"Honey, come quick!" I called to my husband. "Help me!"

He quickly came and carried the little bird (it was actually a fledgling, almost ready to fly) to a protected place in our rock garden and placed him there under a bush. Meanwhile, the parents were frantic, circling and crying their distress.

We went back in the house, but I could still hear the parent robins crying and crying. I remember saying to my husband, "I can't wait to live in a world where no creature hurts another!" Isaiah 11:9 promises that someday that desire will be a reality: "They shall not hurt nor destroy in all My holy mountain" (NKJV).

Dave had to leave to run an errand, so I went out alone to check on the injured bird. I found the crows trying to get at him again, so I stood out there by the rock garden and shooed them away. Of course, the robin parents didn't understand what I was doing, and they kept circling and crying and trying to scare me away! They must have thought that I was one more danger to their baby. But at last the crows gave up and flew high into the sky, so I went into the house to let the parents try to help their baby.

But as I washed sinks and swept floors, all I could think about was that injured bird.

I wanted to go help him but I didn't know what to do. And I kept thinking that he was too badly injured to survive. He was going to die anyway.

Suddenly, God gave me one of those little nudges that He often gives His children. The thought came clearly. *Ginny, that little bird might die anyway if you try to help him, but it will die for sure if you don't help him.*

So I went outside to deliver first aid to a critically injured baby robin. I found him still under the bush, but he had fallen over on his back and lay with his feet straight up to the sky. Kneeling in the grass, I reached out to stroke his soft little body. It was already a little cool. But as I stroked a wing, he suddenly opened his one good eye and struggled weakly to get away. I picked him up to a chorus of cries from his parents, and holding him in my hands to warm him, I took him into the house to try to save his life.

I held him until he was warm, then wrapped him in a piece of an old towel and put a compress on his eye to stop the oozing blood. Then I coaxed him to drink warm water from an eyedropper, stroking his throat until he swallowed. With each swallow, he became stronger and stronger. After half an hour or so, he cuddled down into my hand and willingly opened his beak for the water.

I still didn't know what to do with him, so I called the Audubon Society in Portland. They agreed to take him if I would bring him to them. So on this busy Friday afternoon, I found myself driving across Portland to deliver my patient. All the way there I talked to him, encouraging him; and he chirped back to me, encouraging me. When he became quiet, I would slip the lid off his shoebox and check on him. He would look up at me with his one eye and cock his head back and forth, then cuddle under my hand as I stroked him.

When I got to the Audubon Society building, I put the box in the warmed cage they had waiting for the little fledgling. When the lid was removed, he jumped right out of his box and hopped around his new cage. The Audubon lady smiled and I smiled, and I know that bird smiled. Then she exclaimed, "I think he's going to make it!"

And all I could answer back was, "So do I! So do I!"

There are so many people who, like that little robin, are broken and bleeding. And so often, because I don't understand their situation, it's easy to walk away, to remain detached and uninvolved. It's easy to think that I can't or won't make a difference anyway—so what's the point in trying.

But God keeps giving me little nudges with people as well as with injured baby birds. The words in 1 John 4:21 are clear: "The command that Christ has given us is this: whoever loves God must love others also" (TEV).

Love doesn't walk away.

Love can't remain detached.

Love stays by to make a difference in a lost life.

That little robin never said "thank you" in words I could understand. He probably doesn't remember that I snatched him from certain death. He may not even know I introduced him to a woman who had the knowledge and skills to do whatever was needed to be done to restore him to health and productivity.

So would I do it again?

Absolutely! Love saves even where there is no thankfulness.

Of course, you know that I'm not talking just about saving baby birds. It's all about introducing lost people, hurting people, broken people, to the only One who can make an eternal difference in their lives. It happened for me when my dad introduced me to Jesus. Wouldn't you love to be known as the "introducer," the one who brings people to Jesus?

I surely would.

Chapter 8

A Changed Life

From the moment he married my mother, my dad began encouraging us to go visit the Seventh-day Adventist Church, even though he no longer was a member of that church or any church. Finally, he arranged for someone from the Green Lake church in Seattle to come pick us up each Sabbath morning. And so for several months, I went to the Adventist church every Saturday, and every Sunday I went to the Methodist church. I never joined the Methodist church but I attended it because a lot of my friends went there and I could sing in the choir with them.

I have often thought of that family who went out of their way to pick us up and take us to the Green Lake church those few months back in 1953. They never knew that we became Seventh-day Adventist Christians. I don't even know their names. But can you imagine their surprise when we get to heaven? I can hardly wait to tell them, "I was one of those ragged little girls that you took to church." I think God has some marvelous surprises for us in heaven.

When we moved to a small town in Iowa at the end of the custody battle, there were no nearby Adventist churches. Two years later, we moved to Omaha, Nebraska, where there was an Adventist church. But by then church didn't seem very important to me. I was so involved in being a teenager that I didn't have time for it. My life was taken up by my friends—ball games and dances on Friday nights, shopping and movies on Saturdays, parties and dating, and all the rest. Now I am thankful that my parents were quite strict, though I wasn't thankful then. I had early curfews compared to my friends, and I never really tried the drinking or smoking that many of my friends were just beginning to do.

Still my dad would frequently tell us, "You ought to visit the Adventist church."

We moved to Chicago in November of my high school sophomore year. And our very first Saturday in Chicago, my dad casually asked if we'd like to visit the Adventist church. We hadn't been in town long enough to register at Austin High School, where we would be going, so we knew no one. No dates or ball games yet! We agreed to go to church.

From the moment I walked into that church, I knew my heart had found its home. It was not a pretty church. Rather, it was a low, squat building designed by an apprentice of Frank Lloyd Wright. Called the old West Central Church, it was located on the west side of Chicago just a few blocks from Oak Park. A few years later, they built a beautiful new church in Oak Park. But even as a teenager, I discovered the truth that it's not the outward beauty of the building that is important. It's the beauty *inside* the church that changes lives. We began taking Bible studies, and in April we went to the evangelistic meetings being held there. And with my dad's encouragement, my mother, my sister, and I were baptized on a beautiful spring day in 1957.

When I look at my life, at everything that happened, only my sister knows what it was like for me. Even my mother doesn't know—she wasn't there for all those long, terrible weekend visits. But my sister and I went through it all together. My sister, my precious sister. Together we vowed that we would never be like our father. Together we vowed that we would never drink. Together we promised to follow Jesus.

"My sheep listen to my voice;
I know them, and they follow me"
(John 10:27).

The decision to follow Jesus was easily the most important decision of my life. It was also the most life-changing. That decision influenced every important decision I have considered since then. My life work, the man I would marry, my friendships, and even what I would read, watch, and listen to—all had to be filtered through the decision to let God be in control of my life.

Several years ago, when my granddaughters were much younger, we were listening to children's Bible songs as we rode along in the car, and an old song that many of us grew up with began to play. We sang along with the words:

> One door and only one
> And yet its sides are two.
> I'm on the inside,
> On which side are you?

When it ended, Ashley, who was a little more than six years old, said to me, "Mimi, do you know what that song means?"

"Yes, I do," I told her.

She responded, "Let me tell you what I think it means."

"OK," I said. "Do! Go ahead."

"It means that Jesus is knocking at the door of our hearts, and we have to decide to answer the door or not. He can't come in unless we open the door."

She went on very seriously, "See, there are two sides. There's God's side and there's Satan's side. We have to choose which side we want to be on. We have to choose to be on God's side or Satan's side. And Mimi," she said, "I have already made up my mind. I have given my life to Jesus. I love Him very much, and I choose to be on God's side."

Quick as wink, before I could say anything, Kennedy, who was about three years old, waved her little hand in the air to get our attention. Then she shouted out, "OK, then I'll be on Satan's side!"

Ashley was absolutely horrified and told her little sister very emphatically, "You can't do that!"

"OK," Kennedy replied meekly. "Then I'll be on God's side."

We laugh when we hear that story because we realize that Kennedy did not understand what she was choosing. In her young mind, she reasoned that if you were on one side, then she would be on the other. That's what she knew of how games were played. Obviously, she did not realize the deep significance of the choices we all make.

Your life story is the story of which side you choose to be on, the story of who you choose to serve. The Bible is full of stories of men and women who made their choices, and we can easily see how those choices affected their lives. The old saying that hindsight is always 20/20 is true, but we don't have the luxury of hindsight when we make our decisions. Perhaps that is why it's so vital to make the decision to follow Jesus because that decision will guide in all the other decisions we will make.

In his old age, Joshua, a leader of all Israel, brought together the heads of all the tribes of Israel and reminded them of their history and how God had led and protected and even fought for them throughout their history. He concluded with the challenge, "You must choose for yourselves today whom you will serve. . . . As for me and my family, we will serve the LORD" (Joshua 24:15, NCV).

That's my choice too. What about you?

Chapter 9

God Plans My Life

For many people, Chicago is just another big city. But for me, that city will always be a bit magical. Three of the most important events in my life happened in Chicago. First, it was here that I found Jesus when I was fifteen years old. My sister and I were attending Austin High School on the west side of Chicago. Austin was a very large public high school with about four thousand students. She was a junior, and I was a sophomore. After we were baptized in May of that school year, I spent my next two years of high school at Broadview Academy, a Christian boarding school.

The second event happened in the summer of 1962. I met David Allen three years earlier when we were both freshman at Andrews University in Berrien Spring, Michigan. We started dating in March of that freshman year. We were friends who fell in love. First we liked each other; then we loved each other. A good formula. Two years later, when I was a senior nursing student at Hinsdale Sanitarium and Hospital and David Allen was a senior at Andrews University, came that second event. On my birthday that warm summer in 1962, he asked me to marry him.

The third was our wedding in the summer of 1963 at the Hinsdale, Illinois, church. For us, the fairy-tale ending is turning out to be true—we have "lived happily ever after." But between the second and third events, something happened that truly changed the course of both of our lives.

Almost every weekend Dave got in his little red Karmann Ghia and drove to see me at Hinsdale. It was a Friday evening in the late fall of 1962, and we were sitting across the table from each other eating supper in the hospital cafeteria. He leaned across the table, took both of my hands in his, and asked me a question.

"Honey, how would you like to marry a minister?"

Now let me explain something. As I was growing up, my family moved around a lot. I went to thirteen different schools in my twelve years of schooling. I had lived in ten different towns and six different states. My husband had the opposite experience. His family was from LaPorte, Indiana. Five generations of Allens had lived in this beautiful little town about ninety miles from Chicago. The thought of putting down roots and being an Allen from LaPorte had great appeal to me.

The Allens never moved. In fact, his folks moved into their home the day they brought the newborn baby, who became my husband, home from the hospital, and they stayed in that same house for the next fifty-seven years. It was sold a few years after Dad Allen died. Grandma Nana Allen moved into her house as a young bride and stayed until she was more than ninety. Dave and I had already picked out the spot in LaPorte where we wanted to build our home. I knew ministers often moved around a lot. I also knew that my future husband was planning to go into the family business. He was not planning to be a preacher.

So when he asked me that question—"Honey how would you like to marry a minister?"—I told him, "Oh, no! I could never do that."

He looked very startled and he let the subject drop. At breakfast the next morning, he very casually, but earnestly, asked the same question. "Honey, how would you like to marry a minister?"

Again I told him No, but this time I added a few things. I told him, "A minister's wife needs to be quiet and dignified and needs to know how to play the piano. I'm not very quiet or dignified and I don't play the piano!"

He changed the subject, and we talked about other things.

That noon again in the cafeteria, he leaned over, took both of my hands in his, and asked me once more, "Honey, how would you like to marry a minister?" But this time he didn't give me a chance to answer. He quickly added, "I feel that God is calling me into ministry."

I thought very deeply for about three seconds before I replied, "I would love to marry a minister."

So we were the Allens who never lived in La Porte, Indiana. God had a different plan for our lives.

> *"I know the plans I have for you, says the Lord.*
> *They are plans for good and not for evil,*
> *to give you a future and a hope"*
> (Jeremiah 29:11, TLB).

I can't tell you how many times I sat in the window of my room in the nurses' dorm at Hinsdale and watched for Dave's little red and white Karmann Ghia to come around the corner. Because he was a student at Andrews University in Michigan while I was a nursing student in Hinsdale, near Chicago, we were more than a hundred miles apart during the week. He wrote almost every day, and I wrote nearly as often. In our letters we shared our ideas and plans as well as how we felt about each other. Those love letters were a visible sign of his love for me. He often ended his letters with, "I'll see you this weekend, darling."

From the moment I read those words until he drove up, my heart sang in happy anticipation. I could hardly wait for the weekend. I counted the days and the minutes until we would be together again. I wore his favorite outfits. I re-read my favorites of his love letters to me. My mind was bubbling with thoughts of him and things I wanted to tell him.

Then I would sit in my window on Friday afternoon waiting and watching until I saw his little car coming down the road. By the time he was pulling up, I was at the door to meet him.

We learned the hard way that it was better when we shared our plans. After we were engaged, it was hard to be so far apart. The hundred miles between us seemed like a thousand. So we tried hard to see each other every weekend. One weekend, we had decided we both had too many studies for us to get together. But oh, how I wanted to see him! On Friday morning, a friend mentioned that she was driving over to Andrews and asked if I wanted to go along to see Dave. I decided to surprise him.

We got to the campus at about nine-thirty that night, and I went into the girls' dorm to call him at Shamrock Hall, the honor dorm in which he lived. Our friend Bob Folkenberg answered the dorm phone. Anytime Bob answered the phone he always teased me. I would ask, "Is Dave there?" He'd usually say, "No, he's not here. I just saw him leave with Kathy." Or he'd ask, "Was he expecting you? He told me he was going out with Susie." It was always a different name, whatever came to him at the moment.

So, as usual, he told me, "He's not here."

"Very funny!" I said. "I came all the way from Hinsdale to surprise him."

But Bob said, "No, Ginny, he's really *not* here! He left for Hinsdale a few hours ago. He was going to surprise you!"

After we got together by phone, he turned around and drove all the way back to Andrews that night so we could be together for the weekend. That's the power of love.

Thankfully, God's plans are always what is best for us, plans to give us a future and a hope. That's the power of His love.

I still have all those love letters from Dave. They are very precious to me. They are a part of our history together. When he was at Andrews and I was at Hinsdale, I read them over and over. But I don't read them anymore because we are together all the time. So they sit in a box in the attic, unread but cherished.

———

God gave us the Bible to read over and over until we can be with God all the time. He often wrote that He was coming soon so that our hearts can sing in happy anticipation until He arrives. He is delighted when we watch for Him and wait for Him.

Meanwhile, we have His Word, His love letter to us, to bring us joy and hope in our living, even when we are living in enemy territory. And yes, we are living in enemy territory. Some of you know that too well.

Recently, we were given several boxes of souvenirs from my husband's mother and dad. Among the family treasures, we found hundreds of letters and old postcards written during World War II, while Dad was at Camp Barkeley in Texas and then while he was in France, again during World War II.

As we sat on the floor and read them, it was easy to imagine what it must have been like for Dad to receive them. Mother was a wonderful letter writer. She chatted in great detail about all the things that were happening at home in LaPorte, describing the events of daily life for her and their two little boys. She talked about ordinary things like going to the dairy store to buy milk or how deep the snow was and how many times she got stuck in their long driveway trying to get through to the county road which, thankfully, was plowed. She described the spring flowers along with the weeds that flourished in their good soil. She wrote of their boys kneeling in prayer each night for their daddy. He saw it all through her eyes. And she always told him how much she missed him and loved him.

Dad saved every one of her letters. They gave him a taste of home. They were a reminder of her deep love for her soldier husband. Her love was his hope, his reason for living, while he was literally in enemy territory. The Bible is God's love letter to us. It reminds us of how greatly loved we are. God's love is our hope. It is our reason for living while we are living in enemy territory.

The letters that Dad wrote to Mother were equally full of interesting experiences, but he never described what it was like to be a medic on the battlefield or the trauma he saw in the field hospitals. Instead, his letters were full of his love for her and their two sons, of how he longed to be home, and of how he looked forward to their reunion. The letters were full of plans for their future together when he got home. Once, he even drew up landscaping plans for their little stone house with the big yard.

No wonder they saved every one of their letters.

What a record of their love and commitment during those years that they were separated both by miles and experiences. Many marriages fell apart under those same circumstances. Somehow Mother and Dad were able to keep their hearts united and to focus on their plans for the future. Both of them often shared what God was doing for them and how they trusted Him no matter what. They lived Psalm 37:5: "Commit everything you do to the LORD. Trust him, and he will help you" (NLT). They continually put their plans into His hands, the God they could trust. That was undoubtedly their biggest strength.

Their love, their commitment, their sharing, their trust is a family legacy. It's a legacy that I want to leave for my family too. How about you? What is the legacy you are leaving?

Life Is Good

After Dave finished his studies at the seminary, we moved to Texas to begin our years of ministry. Those years in the great Southwest created wonderful memories. The churches we pastored in various parts of the state are indelibly printed on our hearts. We loved to hear our members introduce us as "our big Yankee pastor and his little wife." I always laughed when they called me "Mrs. Pastor." I loved being a minister's wife. I loved listening to our members and encouraging them in their walk with Jesus. And very soon I loved even more being a young mom. Both our boys were born there in Texas, first Scott, and just fourteen months later, Bob.

Although we loved all of our members, we quickly discovered in our ministry that we especially enjoyed working with teenagers. Our house was always full of teens, and we were happy. So it was not surprising that five years later, my husband accepted a different position in ministry. He became a Bible teacher on the high school level, so he could work all day every day leading young people to Jesus.

We spent the next two years in Southern California at San Gabriel Academy. We had always said we would live any place but Los Angeles, but that is where God placed us. We met amazing young people and made lifelong friends there. It was a good lesson in letting God decide where and how we would serve Him.

Then we spent six years at Laurelwood Academy in the hills outside Portland, Oregon. Our boys started school there. We loved the morning fog on the hills and the thick trees on those same hills. Our boys loved to play in the dense woods. They rode their small trail bikes everywhere and especially enjoyed riding up and down the old sawdust piles left from logging camps. They couldn't hurt themselves when they fell in the soft sawdust.

One summer, they spent days dragging home logs from the woods, attaching them to the back of their trail bikes. With a little bit of help from their dad, they used the logs to build a raft. We took it to the newly created Hagg Lake for the maiden voyage. Standing proudly on the banks, I watched as they launched that big raft. I was still watching when moments later the raft slowly sank. Those were good years too.

Auburn Academy near Seattle, Washington, was next on God's agenda for our lives. Dave was happy in his work of teaching Bible, and I enjoyed my work as the school nurse for this large boarding school. Our boys were growing and completed their high school years there at Auburn. Again, life was good during those eight years, and we made more friends that have stayed in our lives and in our hearts.

The next and last move found us in Vancouver, Washington, across the river from Portland, Oregon. Here we have lived for the past twenty-seven years. At last I have been able to put down roots, and my heart loves living here. Dave taught at Columbia Adventist Academy for eighteen years before he retired a few years ago. I have often heard him say that he has spent his life doing the two things that he most loved to do: sharing God's Word as a teacher and being with teenagers. And then he adds, "And to think that I got paid to do it. What a job!"

After my years of working as a school nurse in our denomination's school system, I found myself working in public schools until I retired at the same time Dave retired. It was a new world for me, and I found I especially loved working with troubled teens. My heart was drawn to the gang members, the teen moms, the kids who struggled with addictions, and especially to those teens whose lives were so painful that they no longer wanted to live. Those suicidal students became my special ministry in my work.

During these years, after my children were grown, God had also called me to a speaking ministry. As I traveled around the United States and many places overseas, I was humbled and filled with awe that God could and would use a woman like me to spread His good news. I agree with Acts 4:20: "We cannot be quiet. We must tell people about what we have seen and heard" (ERV).

I have no pedigree, no seminary diploma. I am not a theologian. I am just a small, funny woman who has a heart for God. My greatest joy comes from my relationship with Jesus. What a privilege to share what is most precious to me. I want my life to be a tribute to God, who so carefully planned such happiness for me. I remind myself every day that I am His much loved child.

None of us saw the coming heartache.

"The Lord will not forsake his people,
for they are his prize"
(Psalm 94:14, TLB).

The discovery that you are a child of God is to see yourself with new eyes. It changes how you view yourself. It gives you a new perspective on your value, your worth. It is a discovery that never leaves you, a discovery that you hold close to your heart as you let the significance wrap you in arms of love.

One day many years ago, I was shopping at Value Village. I don't know if you have Value Village in your area, but it is a bit like Goodwill. You can find a few treasures there if you are willing to poke through a lot of stuff.

I was looking though the stuffed animals for a project that I was planning. Most of them were pretty grubby and ragged. But then I saw a white foot sticking out from the top shelf, a clean white foot. I pulled it down and knew immediately that I had found a "good" bear. He was made out of authentic mohair, not just polyester. He had a hump on his back like a little grizzly bear, and when I turned him over, he made a *baw* sound just like a real baby bear.

Under his armpit I found a little label that read "HERMANN-Teddy-Original, Made in West Germany." The price tag in his ear said $2.98, but it was two-for-the-price-of-one that day so I bought some other little animal, and the bear ended up costing just $1.50. I assumed he would have some value since he was from West Germany.

When I took him home, I showed him to my husband and then placed him on a chair in the family room. But I was curious about my little white bear.

One day several weeks later, I was at the library and saw a book on collectibles. I looked up the teddy bear section and there I found HERMANN teddys from West Germany. They are comparable to the better known Steiff teddy bears. Most surprising of all was the value of my little bear. At that time he was worth between $250 and $350 dollars. His value has increased greatly since then.

I went right home and took him out of the family room and placed him on the best antique chair in the living room, where he still sits today in his place of honor! Several bear collectors who have heard this story or seen the bear have asked if they could buy him. I always tell them that there is a little invisible sign in front of my bear that reads "NFS."

Do you know what that means? NFS stands for "Not For Sale!" My little bear is not for sale.

I think God has a little invisible sign in front of each one of us. Do you know what it says?

Yes! It reads "NFS!"

Sometimes we feel like the little bear on the shelf, alone, neglected, overlooked, with no one who recognizes our real value. But God knows not only where we are, He also knows our worth. He knows the price that was paid for you and for me because He paid it! First Corinthians 7:23 says, "You were bought at a price" (NKJV). I like the way another version says it so plainly: "You have been bought and paid for by Christ, so you belong to him" (TLB).

That's the good news today! Jesus loved you so much that He was willing to do whatever it took to save you. He paid the price for your life by giving His own life on the cross. If ever we doubt our value to God, all we have to do is look at the Cross. The Cross shows what we are worth to God.

That, friends, is the good news today and forever. You are loved! You are valued! You are God's prize! You are God's special treasure. And He will never give you up. If you could see it, you would find a little sign in front of you. It reads "NFS," and it is written by God's own hand and signed by His Son, Jesus.

Chapter 11

Things Don't Matter

In January 2002, my husband bought me a new-to-us car. The car I had been driving was ten years old and had lots of miles on it. We keep our cars a long time, so this was a big decision.

I don't particularly enjoy car shopping. I'm not really that interested in cars. I just want the car to look nice, be the right color, and have lots of little buttons that make things go up and down. Oh, and because I like words, the name has to sound right.

I like for my husband to shop around and narrow the choices to three or four cars, and then let me pick from those. But this time I went with him to find a car. In fact, we spent part of our Christmas vacation car shopping, and the first week in January we found the perfect car. Low miles, only a year old, and it had a nice name—Buick LeSabre. Best of all, it was silvery blue and had lots of little buttons to push. I loved it!

The fourth time I drove it, I was on my way to work and stopped at a red light. As I sat there minding my own business, all of a sudden I heard that awful crunching sound of metal on metal, and my car was slammed slightly forward. I remember exactly what I thought! *I can't believe this! I have had this car for only four days! That's all—four days!* The other driver and I both turned the corner and pulled over to the side of the street.

A woman jumped out apologetically. "I'm so sorry. I thought you were going to turn right on red."

"A car was coming," I told her.

"I know!" she cried. "I saw it after I hit you."

I was not happy as I drove on to my assigned school. I called my husband with my sad tale. I must admit my car had very little damage. In fact, there were just two scratches where the bolts on her license plate had hit my bumper. But I well remember how I felt.

That was Thursday morning. Two and a half days later, the car that was the perfect color with all the little magic buttons did *not* matter in any way at all, and it still doesn't.

You see, two and a half days later, my son, our younger child, was dead.

"As for me, I trust in You, O Lord;
I say, 'You are my God.'
My times are in Your hand"
(Psalm 31:14, 15, NKJV).

Life is full of ordinary days. Days that don't seem to be significant at the time. It is only in retrospect that we see the lesson. Things are, in the end, just things. They have no value in comparison to what matters most in life.

One day I had an errand at the main office in the school where I work. As I turned into the office door, I ran right into a rotund little man coming from the office into the hall. He had a red flower in his lapel and gray sideburns with a fancy gray mustache that twirled and curled on the ends. He looked so familiar to me that I was sure I knew him. But in the brief moment when I was bouncing off his tummy, I just couldn't place him.

Now the sanguine personality in me took over, as it usually does, and I smiled and said to him, "Hi, how are you?"

He responded warmly, although he looked a little puzzled. "Well, hi! I'm just fine. How are you?"

And still exuding sanguine warmth and cheer, I replied, "Fine! I'm fine! Busy as usual, but happy."

Now he was looking very puzzled, but he answered, "Good!"

I was sure this fellow must be a friend, he looked so very familiar, so

I continued, "Listen, I've got a lot to do, but why don't you stop by my office sometime, and we can have a little chat? It's good to see you. Take care!"

He replied in a very puzzled tone, "*Weeeelll,* OK. See you!"

As I went on into the office, I looked back. He had stopped and was looking back at me with a very, very puzzled expression.

Suddenly, I realized that he was being followed. Right behind him strode the superintendent of education for Portland Public Schools, who at the time was Dr. Matthew Prophet. Next to him was the principal of our school, George Galati. Following them were the three vice principals from our school, the two security guards from our school, a uniformed city police officer, two or three folks wearing the green jackets that identified them as part of Portland's Gang Task Force, and last of all came three men carrying large video cameras on their shoulders. The cameras were marked Channel 2, Channel 6, and Channel 8.

It was at that moment that I realized I had just invited Bud Clark, who was then the mayor of Portland, to stop by my office and have a little chat!

You see, I had seen this man so many times on television that I thought I knew him. I had heard his voice on both TV and the radio. I had seen his picture in newspapers. I thought I knew him, but at the crucial moment, I couldn't quite place who he was in my life.

And by the way, he never did come by my office for that little chat.

It was later that same day, when I was telling my husband about this experience and he was laughing at me, that I realized sometimes, as Christians, we treat God the same way that I treated Bud Clark. We hear so much about Him, we've seen so many pictures of Him that we think we know Him. We're familiar with who He is, we may even talk a lot about Him, but we know Him only secondhand. We don't know Him personally. And then sometimes at the crucial moments of our lives, we can't quite remember who He is because we don't know Him personally. And when we run into Him, we make small talk and hurry on our way because we can't quite place Him in our lives.

I want to tell you that it's not enough to talk about Jesus, we must talk to Him.

It's not enough to know about Jesus, we must know Him.

It's not enough to simply recognize His picture. We must know who He is in our lives.

Second Timothy 1:12 says it emphatically: "I know whom I have believed" (NKJV).

God wants us to know with absolute certainty who He is in our lives. He wants us to slow down and take time to know Him. He wants us to quiet our hearts and the rush and noise of the world so that we can know Him.

I think that is what Psalm 46:10 means: "Be still, and know that I am God" (NKJV).

It doesn't say to think or hope or discuss or imagine or debate. The verse says with certainty, "*Know* that I am God."

This is not just an option in the life of the Christian. Most of us like choices. We like to decide what we will do, what we will wear or see or hear or eat and more. And that's usually a good thing. Because we are all so different in our God-given personalities, we make different choices.

But what we're talking about here is not just another option. It is not one choice among many. The choice to know God is truly a salvation issue. Remember these words of Jesus recorded in John 17:3: "This is eternal life, that they may know You, the only true God, and Jesus Christ whom You have sent" (NKJV).

When you know Him, everything that happens in your life can be filtered through His love for you. It makes a difference.

In fact, it makes all the difference in the world.

Chapter 12

Bad News

My husband and I had gone that weekend in January to our denomination's youth camp at Big Lake in the mountains of central Oregon. This annual church winter outing at Big Lake was a part of our family tradition. By now our two sons were married. The beautiful Christian girls they picked as their wives perfectly completed our family. Usually, we were all together for this winter trip. But this year, although our younger son, Bob, and his wife, Dana, were there with their little girls, our older son, Scott, and his wife, Cathie, didn't come because they were busy getting ready to move into their new house.

Saturday night a group of young adults went out to ride snowmobiles on the logging roads around the camp. It was dark, crisp, and clear with the usual deep mountain snow. My husband and I stayed back in the lodge to watch over our granddaughters while we played games with our friends.

It was around eight-fifteen on Saturday night, and I was upstairs in our room where I had just changed Kennedy into her pajamas.

Dana's cousin came running into the room. He was out of breath but calm as he said, "There's been an accident. Bob is out. We need Dave."

My husband grabbed his snow clothes, ran out, and jumped on the back of a departing snowmobile, and headed to the scene of the accident.

Now to a nurse, the word *out* often means simply that someone has been knocked out. I have heard that expression many times in my work as a school nurse. I fully expected that when Dave arrived, our son would jump up. In my mind, I could hear him saying, "Oh, Dad, I'm OK! You didn't have to come."

When I went downstairs, everyone was standing around in little groups, a bit worried but not panicky. Everything had happened so fast that none of us really knew what was going on. We prayed as a group that everything would be all right.

My granddaughters were there and picking up bits and pieces of what was being said. Kennedy at two-and-a-half didn't understand, but I could see the worry beginning to form in Ashley's eyes. She was five-and-a-half and could well understand that her daddy had been in an accident. My friend Bonnie took the girls aside and entertained them for the next few hours while we waited for news. She kept them from the fear that was beginning to envelop my heart.

I can remember almost every moment of those next four-and-a-half hours, yet it all seems like a blur. As the minutes, and then hours, passed, a number of friends would say to me, "It must be good news because it's taking so long."

I didn't tell them, but in my heart I knew it was the opposite. I kept thinking that if it were good news, surely someone would have come by now to tell me.

"God is our refuge and strength, a very present help in trouble. Therefore we will not fear"
(Psalm 46:1, 2, NKJV).

We all want good news. Sometimes people jokingly ask, "Do you want the good news first, or do you want the bad news first?" The truth is we don't want the bad news at all. We want our lives to be full of the people and the things that make us happy. We don't line up for bad news. In fact, our hearts almost stop when we hear those words—bad news.

Once when I was in Australia, my friend Carol Ferch-Johnson and I went to downtown Sydney to shop and see the sights, taking the train from Wahroonga, where she lived, into the city. We shopped in the Queen Victoria Building, explored Darling Harbor, where I tasted pavlova for the first time, and watched sharks swim over our heads in the Sydney aquarium. When we finally headed home on the train, I was tired but happy.

We got off at the Hornsby Station so Carol could buy a few groceries before her husband picked us up at an agreed upon spot. It was a bit crowded at the station, so Carol was a little ahead of me as she went through the turnstile. When my turn came, I made sure the arrow on the ticket was lined up in the right direction. Then I pushed it into the little slot and waited three seconds for the red gate arms to open. Instead, out popped my ticket with a daunting message. "Invalid."

"Now how can this be?" I said to myself.

I thought maybe I put my ticket in upside down. So I carefully lined it up, pushed it in the slot, and out it popped again. "Invalid." I looked up and saw that Carol was already standing on the other side of the gates, in complete freedom, I might add. So I'm thinking that since we bought our tickets together, it can't be my ticket that is bad. It must be that this turnstile is defective. I moved over to the next one. In went my ticket and back came the message, "Invalid."

My thinking switched to fast-forward. My thoughts flew from something about security men and passports to how I was going to explain to my husband back home in Vancouver that I was trapped forever in the Sydney train system to wondering if I could just climb over the little red gates. But out of the corner of my eye, I could see a guard standing just a few feet away letting people through a special gate. I thought he might not be too excited if he saw me climbing over the gates. Then it occurred to me that he might actually be very excited! So instead, I just went over and handed him my ticket and said, "This thing won't work."

I was still thinking it had to be the system. It couldn't be my ticket because I was with Carol and she lived here and knew the system. She bought the tickets, so obviously I did everything right. It had to be the turnstile or something else in the system.

The security guard looked at my ticket and said, "Lady, it won't work because it's invalid."

I looked out and there was Carol standing a few feet away in total freedom, smiling sweetly. Now I didn't know whether to involve her or not. What if they discovered her ticket was invalid too, and we both wold be stuck? I rapidly discarded those chivalrous thoughts, exclaiming, "Well, my friend's ticket worked, and we bought them together."

He looked right at me and explained slowly so I would be sure to understand, "Lady, this ticket is to Wahroonga and this is Hornsby."

That meant very little to me except that a headline flashed through my mind, "American woman jailed! Tried to use bad ticket!" That did it. I quickly said, "I'm with her," and pointed straight at Carol.

Now Carol had two choices. She could walk off and pretend she never knew me, or she could do what she did. She came over and said, "We're together." She showed him her ticket, said a few more things, which I didn't catch because all I was thinking by now was that I wanted out. Then he opened the gates, and I bolted through in case he changed his mind.

"We're together."

Magic words. Gate-opening words.

"We're together." Those words were saying, "She's with me. I'll take responsibility for her. I know she's a foreigner, and she doesn't talk right or do other things just right. But she's with me. We're together."

I had already told the man that I was with her. But my words meant nothing. It wasn't until she claimed me that he opened the gate.

Jesus is already on the other side of the gates. He's been through the system. He's been where we are. But now He's on the other side of the gates, waiting for us, smiling encouragingly.

Our tickets are invalid. We can't buy our way in, and we can't talk our way in. We can't even climb in over the gates. All we can say is, "I'm with Him."

Jesus also has two choices. He can say, "I don't know you." That's bad news.

Or He can say those gate-opening words, "We're together."

Those words that say, "She's with me. I know she's a foreigner, and I know she didn't do everything just right, but she's with me. We're together." That's good news.

I love Matthew 25:34 where Jesus says words that open heaven's gates. "Then I, the King, shall say to those at my right, 'Come, blessed of my Father, into the Kingdom prepared for you from the founding of the world' " (TLB).

"Come!" That's a gate-opening word. Welcome to His kingdom!

Chapter 13

The Worst

The hours passed slowly. Around 11:00 P.M., I went upstairs to put my granddaughters to bed. After they were tucked in, we prayed, sending up special prayers for their daddy. Then Kennedy asked me to sing to her. At that time, she was saying "h" for "s" so it came out, "Hing a hong, Mimi." We were always Papa and Mimi to our precious grandgirls.

Earlier that day when I put her down for a nap, Kennedy was mad that she had to sleep while everyone else was playing, and she had told me emphatically, "No hinging, Mimi!" Now she wanted me to "hing a hong." So I "hang a hong," and very soon she was asleep.

It was harder for Ashley. She kept thinking about her daddy, and I could see the concern in her green eyes. In a worried voice, she asked me, "Is my daddy OK? Will they have to take him to the hospital?"

I'm so glad I didn't make any promises, even though it is tempting to say what you think someone wants to hear, especially when it is a child. Instead, I told Ashley, "Honey, I don't know. We'll know in the morning when you wake up."

It was just after 1:00 A.M. when I saw the camp caretaker dusted with snow come into the kitchen. I knew he had been at the scene of the accident. I heard someone say, "Ginny, he wants to see you."

And at that moment, I knew without a doubt that my son was dead.

I knew that if it were good news, he would have come out to talk to me along with everyone else, so we all could hear the good news. But when he asked to see me alone, I knew it could not be the good news for which I was praying. As I walked toward the kitchen, I kept thinking of what I had been saying over and over to myself through all those long hours. *If it's the worst, Ginny, you can do this. Your faith is strong. You can do this.*

Then I heard him ask, "Are you Bob's mom?"

"Yes," I whispered.

"I'm sorry to tell you, but your son has passed."

"I weep with grief; encourage me by your word"
(Psalm 119:28, NLT).

Goodbyes are usually not easy. Especially if you know you will not see each other again for some time. As our boys were growing up, we always spent several weeks each summer with their grandparents, our parents, in both Indiana and Missouri. The day we left for home was always hard because we knew it would be a whole year before we saw each other again. After the final hugs and kisses, when we were in the car and ready to begin the long trip home to the Northwest, Mother Allen could hardly stand it. She would quickly reach in for one more hug and then load us up with her favorite sugary snacks as a last gift of love. We never told her that we threw them out at the first stop for gas because none of us liked them, not even our boys. We accepted them as the gift of love she meant it to be. She waved and blew kisses as long as we were in sight.

In April 2008, I was in Michigan for several weekends speaking for a Christian women's retreat. I spent the week days in between the retreats visiting family in La Porte, Indiana. And, of course, this included my mother-in-law, who was in a nursing home connected with the La Porte Hospital. Mother Allen had suffered from Alzheimer's for many years, and for the last few years she did not recognize even her children most of the time. She was also a double amputee, so her life had not been good for several years.

My precious mother-in-law had loved to be out of doors. She was never happier than when she was working in her yard, and truly it was magnificent. She could make anything grow. It was not uncommon for her to plant more than a hundred flats of flowers in her yard, and once the Allen yard was featured in a magazine for its beauty. I used to tell her that she had such a green thumb that if she had watered her windowsills, they would have sprouted and bloomed.

So it was heartbreaking to see her confined to a wheelchair.

It was a warm spring day, and the early flowers and blossoming trees delighted my senses when I went in to see her. It was the kind of day she loved to be barefoot, always barefoot, in her yard. I found her sleeping in her bed in the small room that held no spring delight for her. This small room knew no change of seasons.

I stood beside the bed and just watched her for a while, softly stroking her white hair. When she finally opened her eyes, I knew she would not know who I was. And sure enough, when she looked up at me, I saw the familiar confusion in her eyes. She was trying to focus, trying to uncover the memories deeply buried within her once bright mind, she who had been valedictorian of her high school class in Rolling Prairie.

Finally, she frowned a little and turned her head to look at the composite picture of her three boys hanging on the wall at the foot of the bed. She looked at the first picture which was of Bill, the oldest. Then she looked back at me and wrinkling her brow, she questioned, "Bill?"

I knew she was trying to figure out if I belonged to Bill. Somehow she realized that wasn't right.

So she looked back to the picture to the center where she saw Jack, her youngest. His picture was slightly smaller, so it was in the center. Bringing her eyes back to me, she frowned again and said, "Jack?"

No, she knew that wasn't it.

Again focusing on the picture, this time her eyes fell on Dave's face, the middle son, my husband. Looking quickly back to me, her eyes lit up and she said with joy in her voice, "Dave!" She couldn't quite place who I was, but she knew that I belonged to Dave. And because I belonged to Dave, I belonged to her too. I held her hand and told her that I loved her.

What a precious moment that was!

But as quickly as the moment came, it was gone, and I saw blankness and confusion settle back into her eyes. I didn't know it then, but that was my farewell message to my much-loved mother-in-law. And it was her farewell message to me. She died just a few weeks later. I cherish that memory.

------·--·------

That was in April. Just a few short months later in September, I said another farewell. I had just finished speaking at a Christian women's retreat weekend in Atlanta, Georgia, and was spending a few days sightseeing with my good friend Carolyn Karlstrom in the beautiful South. My sister called to tell me that my mother wasn't doing well and had possibly had a stroke. I drove from Atlanta to Tampa, Florida, to be with my mom for her last four days of life.

On the night she died, the rest of the family went to bed, and I sat alone with her. At first I wondered why they would all go to bed when I had told them that it wouldn't be long. But as I sat there alone with my mother, holding her hand, talking to her, singing to her, praying for her, I found I was glad to be alone with her. There was something infinitely sweet that in the end it was just mother and daughter alone together, waiting for the end of her earthly life and knowing that there was an eternity together in her future.

We often hear of a mom or a dad who knows death will be soon, and so they leave a video diary or a written diary for their children. The messages in those diaries are things that the mom or dad want their children to know forever. They are messages for the future to give them guidance, encouragement, and hope.

And they are messages of love, usually repeating again and again how much they love those who are watching or reading.

Farewell messages are important. They are meant to be read time after time. They are meant to give comfort, encouragement, and hope when the days and weeks and then the years stretch endlessly ahead.

They are meant to be held close to the heart.

Jesus, too, had a farewell message for the ones He loved. He knew that His time was short. And so He encouraged His followers with this message: "Don't let your hearts be troubled. Trust in God, and trust also in me. There is more than enough room in my Father's home. If this were not so, would I have told you that I am going to prepare a place for you? When everything is ready, I will come and get you, so that you will always be with me where I am" (John 14:1–3, NLT).

In the summer of 1977, our older son, Scott, decided that he wanted to spend a few weeks in Indiana with Grandpa and Grandma Allen. We always spent several weeks there every summer in Dave's hometown, so Scott knew that we'd be coming a few weeks later to get him. He didn't know exactly when we were coming, but he knew it would be sometime in July around his twelfth birthday.

We set out driving. We called him often and told him where we were so he could keep track of our progress. Finally, we called and told him we would arrive sometime the next day, probably in the early afternoon. He was excited. He had missed his younger brother, Bobby, probably more than he missed us.

As the sun began to set, my husband decided to drive through the night. He missed his boy too much to wait a moment longer. He just wanted to get there.

When we finally arrived, it was about two o'clock in the morning. Other years when we had arrived during the night, we had napped in the driveway until morning, not wanting to wake anyone up. But this time Dave couldn't stand to wait. We raced to the house, and he ran right to Scott, waking him up with a big hug.

Scott looked up with sleepy eyes and said to his daddy, "I knew you would come in the night. I knew you couldn't wait 'til morning. I just knew you would come in the night."

In His farewell message, Jesus took time to pray for His followers.

He prayed, "Father, I want these people that you gave me to be with me where I am" (John 17:24, NCV). He wants to be with you. Remember His earlier words, "I will come and get you, so that you will always be with me where I am." He's coming! We are living in the night season for this world. He can hardly wait.

The last prayer of the Bible, found in Revelation 22:20, echoes the cry of our hearts, "Even so, come, Lord Jesus" (NKJV).

Hold His words close to your heart. The promise is for you. He was thinking of you when He gave His farewell message.

Chapter 14

The Longest Night

I remember every detail of that night. The absolute crushing pain as I cried over and over, "My baby! My baby! My son!" Every mother knows that for as long as she lives, when her children need her, they are always her "baby." I remember seeing my husband and daughter-in-law, Dana, come into the lodge kitchen about half an hour later. Holding them and crying together. Calling Scott and his wife, Cathie, knowing what those terrible words were doing to them. Persuading them not to come to Big Lake because it was snowing again and the roads were snowy and slick. I couldn't stand the thought of another accident.

It was the longest night of my life. Trying to get Dana warm after all those hours she had spent at the accident site. She had sat in the snow, cradling the head of her lifeless husband while my husband simply held her. Five hours in the falling snow. Waiting for the paramedics to arrive. More waiting for the coroner to come and officially pronounce him dead. Then even more waiting—for the sheriff to arrive to investigate the circumstances. Finally, the trip to the parking lot on snowmobiles, following Bob's tarp-covered body, which was carried on a sled.

Later trying to sleep knowing that sleep was impossible. Every time one of us would turn over or get up to the bathroom, we would touch hands and hug and cry some more.

The morning only brought more sorrow as Ashley woke up and asked for her daddy. How do you tell a five-year-old such devastating news? I don't ever want to see that look on her face again. Her little body crumpled forward, her head low as the tears filled her eyes, and her first words were, "But who will pick me up from school? My dada always picked me up."

We promised her that one of us—her mama, her mimi, her papa, or her other grammie—would always be there to pick her up from school. We have kept that promise. Kennedy was simply bewildered by it all. Her little face was shadowed with sadness as she sensed that something was terribly wrong, but she didn't quite know what it was.

> *The Lord is near to those who have a broken heart.*
> *And He saves those who are broken in spirit*
> (Psalm 34:18, NLV).

A promise made should be a promise kept. How glad we can be that God always keeps His promises. When we go through the darkest of the dark days, when our hearts are crushed with unyielding pain, when we don't see even the tiniest glimmer of light at the end of the tunnel, we don't have to wonder where God is in our lives. The Bible says it clearly: "The Lord is near to those who have a broken heart." It bears repeating. Keep those words in your heart. How often I hear people ask, "Where was God when I needed Him most?"

I know exactly where He is when we need Him most. He is right here. He is near.

Our lives changed in every way after that heartbreaking day.

———

Among other things, now I have the privilege of taking Bob's girls to buy presents for their mom for special occasions. This is something their daddy would normally have done, but after his death, it fell to me. Since my shopping genes are prolific and polished, I love it!

When we first started this tradition, they were young and didn't understand the nuances of shopping. The price was immaterial to them. Whether it cost one dollar or a thousand simply wasn't an issue. Like the time Ashley told me, "We could buy Mom a new car. That would be fun."

I agreed that it would be fun, but we didn't buy her a new car.

By the time they were seven or eight years old, they had learned to look for the sale signs. They knew that if it said "50 percent off," it cost only half of what was marked on the tag. And they understood that it is better to buy something well-made for half price than something cheap for full price—even if the money comes out the same.

They learned to think about what their mom would like rather than what they would like to have. Hinting helped a lot. "Kennedy, I know that dolly is really cute, but let's try to think of the last time Mama picked out a doll for herself. What does she like to do in her spare time? You're right, Ashley, she would probably rather play ball."

When the gift was finally picked out, we found a cashier. And, taking turns, one of the girls solemnly handed my credit card to the clerk. Sometimes the clerk had observed our selection process and helpfully asked, "Who's paying?"

I wish you could have seen the sparkle in those green eyes and hear the pride in the words as each girl, when it was her turn, said, "I am!" and handed over the credit card. My credit card.

I know that they knew that in reality I was paying. But I'm also sure that they never thought about the bill that comes at the end of the month. In the joy of the moment, they forgot who was really paying the price for their gift.

I don't know how it is for you, but I can tell you that for me sometimes, maybe even most of the time, life gets busy. And along with some stress, a little concern, and an occasional tear, there is still mostly happiness. I can also tell you that sometimes in the joy of the moment, I may forget who really paid the price. Sometimes I fail to remember what my moments of joy cost. Sometimes I neglect to think of who paid the price for the choices I make.

The old gospel song says, "Jesus paid it all. All to Him I owe; sin had left a crimson stain, He washed it white as snow."

No money owed. No credit card bill at the end of the month. Just scars in His hands that remind me of the price He paid.

No wonder John wrote, "See how much the Father has loved us! His love is so great that we are called God's children—and so, in fact, we are" (1 John 3:1, TEV).

Think about it. Make it real in your mind. You are God's child. Whether you love Him or hate Him, whether you flee from Him or cuddle in His arms, you remain God's child.

As the old hymn says, Jesus did, indeed, pay it all—so we could be part of His family forever. I hope the sparkle in my eyes tells Him that I appreciate the gift more than I can possibly say. Though I try to tell Him, I find that words are simply not enough.

Some days, not very often, I have no words at all. So on those days when it's hard to smile, when I don't quite understand what is happening, when I'm bewildered by life itself, remind me that the price has been paid so I can look for the joy to return. And when you remind me, remind yourself, so we both can relax in His love.

Chapter 15

God Understands

It was in January that we lost our son. Those months following were difficult beyond my ability to express. Every mealtime for the next nine months—from January until the next September—Kennedy prayed, "Dear Jesus, please bring my daddy come home."

I don't know which was worse, hearing her pray that day after day . . . after day . . . after day, or when she finally stopped asking Jesus to bring her daddy home, for then we knew that she now realized he wasn't ever coming home again.

Once we were at a park when a fire truck arrived. The firemen were just taking a break to stretch a bit. Before we could stop her, Kennedy flew on her tiny feet to the ladder truck. Her daddy had been a firefighter, and she had often seen him in one of the big red trucks. As the men got out of the truck, she ran to each one and looked up, intently studying his face. With hope in her heart, she was looking for her daddy. I saw the hope in her eyes die. Today I close my eyes and I see her walking away from the men, her head hanging, her footsteps slow and measured. My heart once again breaks for her disappointment. How do you explain it all to a little two-and-a-half-year-old child?

Ashley would have an emotional meltdown every few weeks. She would cry inconsolably for her daddy, and nothing we could say or do would help her. It was agony to hear her heart break when she would cry, "I wish I could die! I just wish I could die. Then they could bury me next to my daddy, and we could be together until Jesus comes. Please, Jesus! Just let me die."

Seeing our precious daughter-in-law, Dana, with sadness written over her beautiful features brought more sorrow. The sparkle was gone from her deep blue eyes. Her laughter was gone too. She had tried so hard to save her husband's life by doing CPR for more than half an hour. She had no way of knowing that he had died instantly when he was thrown off his snowmobile and his body hit a tree, rupturing his aorta. More than love, they had cherished each other too. Theirs was a storybook marriage, but it had ended that cold night in the snow.

Eleven months after Bob's death, I drove to the mall to shop for Christmas presents. I pulled into a parking spot, turned off the engine, and suddenly I found myself sobbing uncontrollably, much like Ashley during her hardest times. I couldn't stop crying. I cried so hard I thought I was going to throw up. The pain was so intense I felt as if I couldn't breathe. It was almost an hour later that the tears slowed, and I began to get control. Then I started to pray. I asked, "God, when You lost Your Boy, did You cry so hard You felt as if You were going to throw up?"

In the quietness of my car, I continued, "God, when You saw Your Son on the cross, did You hurt so badly You couldn't breathe?"

Although I did not hear an audible voice, it was as though He answered softly, *"Yes, girlie, I did. I did. I understand."*

During the long months following the death of our child, I prayed more than I have ever prayed in my life. Yet I couldn't get back into the routine of my prayer time. Sometimes I couldn't pray at all. I would just sit and cry. How thankful I am that God understands a broken heart. I think He knew that my tears were my wordless prayer. I know He must have longed to hold me tight and wipe my tears away.

The psalmist's words in Psalm 119:28 were my words: "I weep with grief; encourage me by your word" (NLT). I marked them in my Bible on February 8, almost a month after Bob died. I found it was God's word that encouraged me most. Each day God would lead me to the very verses that I needed at that moment to let me exist.

Little did any of us know what was coming next.

"And now, brothers and sisters, I want you to know what will happen to the Christians who have died so you will not be full of sorrow like people who have no hope"
(1 Thessalonians 4:13, NLT).

I well remember those days when my prayers were filled with tears. I know God remembers them, too, because Psalm 56:8 tells us, "You keep track of all my sorrows. You have collected all my tears in your bottle. You have recorded each one in your book" (NLT).

I am also glad that I have a history with God. I know He remembers not just the tears but also the great joy that my prayer life has brought me through the years. This is the God who created the entire universe, and yet He remembers even the small, joyful moments in my life.

I like to imagine God, the Omnipotent Creator of everything that is and was and ever will be—the Artist who striped the zebra and spotted the leopard, the One who put the song in the canary and the howl in the wolf, who fashioned the fur on the fox and set the velvet nose on the deer, the Astronomer who flung stars into space and hung the northern lights as a curtain of color in His heavens, who created fragrances for flowers so each of us could have our favorite—I like to imagine this wonderful God finding delight in *me*! Somehow knowing that He longs to be with *me* fills my heart with a deep-down joy that is almost indescribable.

Since the invention of cell phones, we are able to connect with anyone anytime, no matter how far away they are. No waiting for a landline. Connection is instantly available.

Much like prayer.

One day when she was about three years old, my younger granddaughter, Kennedy, called me on the phone. When I answered the ring, she whispered, "Hi, Mimi."

"Hi," I replied. "Why are you whispering?"

Her little voice was as quiet and soft as a baby's breath. "Because I'm on a phone time-out. Mama says I call you too much. She says I bother you."

"Well, honey, I don't want you to get in trouble," I told her, "so why don't we hang up and *I'll* call *you*. That way it will be OK, and you won't get in trouble. And, sweetie, you never bother me! I love it when you call."

"OK," she whispered. "But don't forget to call me back." Then she said, very seriously and very softly, "Mimi, I want to talk to you. I need you to call me. I need to talk to you, and I need you to talk to me."

I don't have to tell you what my heart did at that moment. You know I didn't forget to call her back. In just a minute or two I was dialing her number. And we talked. It was nothing earth shattering, just heart-to-heart conversation.

Can you imagine how God would feel if we came to Him in prayer and told Him, "I need to talk to You, and I need You to talk to me"? No wonder God tells us that "the prayer of the upright pleases him" (Proverbs 15:8). Another translation puts it like this: God "delights in the prayers" of His people (NLT).

I have a long phone history with Kennedy. A cool winter day a number of years ago, my husband and I were waiting to get on the SkyTrain in Vancouver, British Columbia, when my cell phone rang. It was so noisy on the train platform that I barely heard the ring.

When I glanced at the screen, I saw that it was not a number I recognized. I figured that for someone to call us in Canada, it must be quite important. Surely whoever was calling knew that it costs a lot to call a cell phone internationally. And the cost is not to the caller but to the cell phone called.

I said "Hello," and in spite of the noise on the platform, I heard a small familiar voice coming from the unfamiliar number. A young, slightly subdued voice said, "Hi, Mimi." It was Kennedy, calling from a friend's phone. I was, of course, wondering what was so important that she had called us in Canada.

The train was pulling in, and the noise greatly increased. So it was a bit inconvenient, which she didn't know. After a few moments of just chatting, she said in a pathetic little voice, "I miss you." Then she had to talk to Papa. They chatted for a few more minutes. Then back the phone came to me for "Goodbye," and "I love you." And yes, we got on the noisy train while she and I were still talking.

Now let me tell you the truth. Was that call expensive? Yes, it was. Was it inconvenient? Yes, it was.

And yes, nothing either of us said was of earth-shattering importance. But when I heard those words, "Hi, Mimi," nothing else mattered. Not the money, not the inconvenience, nothing! This was my girl, and she wanted to talk to me. I held her sweet words, "I miss you," as a treasure in my heart.

Kennedy's call to me was just a little glimpse of what happens in heaven when I call out to God. It's never too inconvenient for Him, and it never costs too much. Through all the noise of all the other voices calling out to God, He hears my voice too. And my words are a treasure held to *His* heart. And maybe when I call and it's not anything special, no big call for help, but just to tell God that I miss Him, maybe, just maybe, that's the greatest treasure of all.

When Ashley was about three years old, Dave and I spent a month in Russia. When we came home, I found a message from Ashley on our answering machine. This is what it said: "Mimi? Papa? This is Ashley Allen. I'm your granddaughter. I just wanted to tell you I love you."

She identified herself in case we didn't remember who she was. As if we wouldn't recognize her voice! I would know that voice anywhere. I love my two granddaughters more than I can possibly tell you. Every time I think of that message, it makes me smile.

And the truth is that God loves *you* more than He can possibly tell you. When He thinks of you, it makes Him smile. His own words recorded in Jeremiah 32:38 tell us how He feels about you and me: "They shall be My people, and I will be their God" (NKJV).

Are you wondering how I know He smiles when He thinks of you? Listen with your heart to Psalm 149:2–4: "Let the children of Zion be joyful in their King. . . . For the LORD takes pleasure in His people" (NKJV). The New International Version says, "The LORD takes delight in his people." And yet another puts it this way: "The LORD is happy with his people" (ERV).

Doesn't that sound to you as if God is smiling? And His smile is for *you.*

Yes, you have an Abba Father, a Daddy, who knows the sound of your voice. Whether your voice is full of tears or full of joy, He will always listen to you. He waits just for you to make the connection.

There are no dropped calls.

No dead spots.

No bad connections.

And it's never out of service.

The line is never busy.

There's not even call waiting.

It's an instant connection.

Just God and you.

That's prayer!

Chapter 16

Bad News Again

Despite our heartache, the months continued to pass. Now it was June. On a warm Saturday evening, my husband and I arrived at a nearby chapel for a family wedding. As I walked through the door, I suddenly felt as if I might throw up. The nausea was so severe that I couldn't stay for the wedding, even though our granddaughters were the flower girls.

The nausea and vomiting continued into the next day, Sunday. We were going to fly to Indiana early Monday morning to spend time with the Hoosier relatives. Dave wanted to cancel the tickets, but I insisted that I'd be feeling better and we should leave as planned.

I should have listened to him. The trip was miserable. When we changed planes in Phoenix, the flight attendant asked me, "Ma'am, should I call the paramedics?"

"No, no, I'll be OK."

He looked at me again. "You don't look so good."

That turned out to be quite an understatement.

By the time we finally arrived in La Porte, I was so sick that my husband slept on the floor by my bed in case I needed something. Each day I was worse. Tuesday. Wednesday. I couldn't eat or drink. Nothing would stay down. I had a high fever, hurt all over, and the pain in my back was excruciating. Dave kept insisting that I go to a doctor, but I insisted that it was just the flu and I would be all right.

On Thursday, I finally agreed to go to the emergency room at the local hospital, if I didn't have to stay. My sister-in-law Cheryl was the hospital supervisor when I arrived. Later she told me that as soon as she saw me, she knew I would not be going anywhere for some time. I still did not realize how sick I was.

Now in the hospital, things moved fast. Several specialists were called in. I was admitted, of course, and several tests, including blood work, CAT scans, and X-rays followed. As the results of the tests started coming in, the news was not good. I had an *E. coli* kidney infection.

My left kidney was nearly 95 percent gangrenous, and the gangrene had started in the right kidney too. The doctors didn't think they could save my left kidney, for it needed to come out in order for me to survive. But I was too sick for them to consider operating. The doctor later told Dave that I was in complete organ shutdown. All of my body systems were failing.

On Saturday afternoon, the doctors told my husband that he had better send for our children if they wanted to see me alive. They weren't sure I would live through the weekend.

> *"You are My servant. I have chosen you*
> *and have not cast you away:*
> *Fear not, for I am with you;*
> *be not dismayed, for I am your God.*
> *I will strengthen you; yes, I will help you"*
> (Isaiah 41:9, 10, NKJV).

When your life hangs in the balance, you weigh what is really important to you. When you're not sure there will be a tomorrow, you look at what is truly important today.

———•◦•———

Does the name Michael Jordan mean anything to you?

One day I was at the airport waiting for someone to arrive when I heard people around me saying, "Look! There are the Chicago Bulls!"

Looking across at the next gate, I saw all these super-tall guys.

Watching them mill about, I casually mentioned to no one in particular that my son really loved basketball and he would have liked to have been there at the airport with me. Someone standing nearby said, "You should go get some autographs for him."

I thought that was a great idea so, not being shy, I trotted over to where they were standing and looked way, *way* up into their faces. Since I am barely five feet tall, it truly was way up.

"Rumor has it that you guys are the Chicago Bulls," I told them.

They laughed and one of them answered, "Rumor has it right!"

I told them about my son (although I didn't mention he was in college!) and said that he would love to have their autographs. So they all started signing the scrap of paper I'd found in my purse. Then one of them pointed to a really, *really* tall guy coming down the concourse toward us. He said, "That's the guy whose autograph you need."

As the really, *really* tall guy came up to us, I told him, "These guys said I need your autograph."

He smiled and added his signature to my little scrap of paper. We chatted a bit, then I thanked them all and went back over to my gate.

A stranger at my gate who had been watching this whole thing came over to me and asked if I had really gotten their autographs.

I answered, "Sure did!"

Then he pointed at the last one, the really, *really* tall one who had signed last, and he asked, "That guy? Did you get his autograph too?"

"Sure did!"

Then, with amazement in his voice, he queried, "Lady, do you know who he is?"

"Sure don't!"

Now I want you to know that today I would recognize Michael Jordan, but that was way back in his very early years as a player. Maybe even his rookie year. He was just starting to be the big name in basketball. So I knew his name but not his face.

The man responded emphatically, "Lady, that's Michael Jordan!"

Then he pulled out his billfold, started counting out money, and said determinedly, "Lady, I'll give you five hundred dollars cash—right now, on the spot—for that autograph."

We all know there are some things that money can't buy, and I knew my son would love having Michael Jordan's signature, so I told him, "No, my son will want this." (However, as I look back on that day, I have often wished that I had taken the money.)

I could hardly wait to call Scott that night at Walla Walla College and tell him I'd gotten Michael Jordan's autograph for him. He was so excited he could hardly wait to come home. He said, "Mom, I'll be home in two weeks to get it!"

But somehow between the time of the phone call and Scott's arrival, I lost Michael Jordan's autograph!

And by the way, that little scrap of paper would have been worth much more today. For most of his career, Jordan rarely signed autographs because of safety concerns. There were too many frenzied fans attempting to get his signature. And sometimes his autograph has been auctioned off for charities for thousands of dollars!

I had been so excited to get that autograph for Scott because I knew he would like it. My intentions were so good, but the autograph was lost in spite of my good intentions. And it was lost, I have to admit, because of my carelessness. Once in a while, all these many years later, my son will still say with a tone of wonder in his voice, "I can't believe my mom had Michael Jordan's autograph and *lost* it!"

I wish I could tell you that the autograph loss was a fluke, a one-time thing, but it brings to mind all too well the four years I spent looking for the pendulum to our antique clock. We were packing for a move from Laurelwood Academy near Portland, Oregon, to Auburn Academy near Seattle, Washington. As I packed, the thought came to me that I should put the pendulum where it would be absolutely safe. And I did. But by the time we started unpacking, I could not remember where that safe place was. I went through everything several times, turning all the empty boxes inside-out, going through packing paper and drawers. I finally resigned myself to the fact that I had probably thrown it out somehow with the packing materials. So the clock sat silent for four years.

Then one day, when I'd gotten a little behind doing laundry, Dave pulled his last clean T-shirt from the dresser drawer. As he unfolded it, out fell the pendulum—where it had been firmly wrapped in the shirt and put in the bottom of the drawer for safekeeping. Again, my intentions had been good, but the pendulum was lost in spite of my good intentions. It was lost because of my busyness on that packing day.

But, in the end, an autograph is just an autograph, and a pendulum is just a pendulum. In the great scope of life, those things really don't matter too much. But can you imagine losing the one thing that matters most in life because of either carelessness or busyness? I can think of no greater tragedy than losing the one thing that really matters to me—my relationship with Jesus. And to lose it because of my carelessness or my busyness is almost unspeakable! Jesus asked, "What will it profit a man if he gains the whole world, and loses his own soul?" (Mark 8:36, NKJV), or as the New Life Version puts it, "What does a man have if he gets all the world and loses his own soul?"

My daily time with Jesus is my way of keeping our relationship strong and healthy. The more time I spend with Him, the better I know Him. The better I know Him, the more I love Him. The more I love Him, the more I trust Him.

Trust is a must-have for any relationship. It cements the love foundation of the relationship. So trust is what keeps me loving Him when I'm not sure where He is leading me. Or why.

There have been quite a few *why*s in my life and a number of *where*s.

I love stories of answered prayers, and I have had more than my share of those. But I find in my life that it is the *why*s and the *where*s that keep my hand most firmly in His. The *why*s and the *where*s are the testing of my trust—trust that is based on our love for each other.

For me, that is what prayer is all about.

Knowing Him.

Loving Him.

Trusting Him.

It wouldn't have changed my life very much if I'd never found the pendulum, and it won't change my life at all if I never find the autograph. What has changed my life immensely and eternally is the decision to do whatever it takes to spend time with Jesus every day. To know Him. To love Him. To trust Him. In the great scope of my life, that's what matters. That's what is really important to me.

Chapter 17

God Knows

The doctors said that *if* I survived through the weekend, on Monday they would decide whether or not to remove my gangrenous kidney. It would be a difficult decision because they still didn't think I could possibly live through the surgery. But they also believed that I could not live unless the kidney was removed.

It was that day that Dave finally realized the seriousness of my situation. Up until then, he simply could not face the fact that he might lose me. He had already lost a son—and now this! That late Saturday afternoon phone call to our older son to tell him of my condition was one of the two hardest calls he has ever had to make. The first was that snowy Saturday night only six months earlier, also to Scott, to tell him that his brother had been killed at Big Lake.

That night Scott and Cathie caught the first flight out from Seattle, where they were visiting friends. I can never express what I felt when they walked into my room early Sunday morning. I knew then that I must be far, far sicker than I thought.

That Sunday morning Dave asked me if I wanted to be anointed. I told him Yes, even though I was too sick to do the heart preparation I would have liked to have done before this holy ceremony. That evening my family gathered around my bed with a pastor friend. They prayed that God would heal me, but they gave Him permission to do whatever He saw best for my life. Then the oil of anointing was placed on my forehead, following the instructions given in James 5:14, 15: "Are any of you sick? You should call for the elders of the church to come and pray over you, anointing you with oil in the name of the Lord. Such a prayer offered in faith will heal the sick, and the Lord will make you well" (NLT).

The next morning there was marked improvement in all the tests, and the doctor told Dave, "This was from above."

The main kidney specialist who took care of me first met Dave in the emergency room. That day he told my husband, "I want you to know I pray for my patients." Now he said, "We didn't do this. God did this."

Thank God for praying doctors!

I have to admit that I don't have all the answers on prayer. I don't know why some people are healed and some are not. I don't know why some live and some die. But I do know how God feels about it: "Precious in the sight of the LORD is the death of his saints" (Psalm 116:15, NKJV). And I do know how God feels about *me*. "You are precious and honored in my sight, and . . . I love you" (Isaiah 43:4). So when we don't know the answers, we can still rest in peace because we know the God who does know the answers.

And so God graciously healed me. I began to slowly get better—slowly, very, very slowly.

"O Lord, my God
I cried out to You, and You healed me"
(Psalm 30:2, NKJV).

I am so glad that God sees the bigger picture in all of our lives. He sees what we do not see. He knows what we do not know. And whatever He does is always for our best good. He doesn't check our family tree. He's not looking for a pedigree. His plans for your life are based not on who you are but rather on what you are. First John 3:1 tells us exactly what we are: "How great is the love the Father has lavished on us, that we should be called children of God! And that is what we are!"

It can't get plainer that that.
You are His much-loved child.

Some years ago, on a warm May afternoon when we were living at Auburn Academy, my doorbell rang. There stood a little girl with a tiny bird in her cupped hands. She had found the bird under a blossoming tree in her yard. She looked for its parents, but they had not come back. Now she asked me if I would keep the bird.

Everyone in the neighborhood knew that I loved animals. I had raised four raccoons, a newborn fawn, a baby squirrel, wild rabbits, and more wild rabbits. But I had never particularly liked birds. I had often said that I loved fur but didn't care much about fins and feathers. But here stood this little girl, asking me to be mother to a bird so young that it had only a bit of fluff where its feathers should be.

Well, I couldn't say no, so I took that bird into my home, and of course you know what happened. I took him straight into my heart too. I fed that baby at least every two hours day and night. You have no idea how often a baby bird wants to eat unless you have been a mother to one.

He was so cute. He was covered with gray fuzz and had a gray beak. His beak was lined with yellow out to the edges, so when he looked up, it looked as if he were smiling with big yellow lips. I called him Bozo because he reminded me of a happy little clown.

When he started getting feathers, I looked in the bird book to find out what kind of bird he was. I was raising a starling! And I loved him. I fed that bird. I played with him. I protected him. And I taught him how to fly. In fact, I taught him everything he knew. How I loved that little bird.

But the first time I took him for a walk perched on my shoulder, I found that the world was not ready for Bozo. Everyone who saw him said things like, "Why do you have that dumb starling?" "He's a nuisance bird." "He's a bad bird." "You should kill him." "He doesn't deserve to live."

One woman even said to me, "Ginny, if I were you, I'd take that bird and throw him down on the cement so hard it would bash his head. That's all he's worth."

They were talking about a bird I loved. This was *my* bird!

I began to worry about releasing him. He had never known anything but kindness from human hands. What would happen to my little bird with the big yellow smile the first time he flew down to some unsuspecting shoulder?

I had heard of the Wild Bird Clinic in nearby Renton, so I decided to call them and ask if they would take Bozo. I had also heard that they released their birds in sanctuaries where they would be safe. But I kept remembering what everyone said about my bird, and I was afraid to tell them that Bozo was a starling. What if they didn't want him either?

When the phone was answered, I explained who I was and then quickly added, "I have a teenage bird that needs a home. He's a really nice bird. Can you take him?"

"I think so," she told me. "What kind of a bird is he?"

The very question I didn't want to hear! I didn't want to tell her. So I started talking faster. "He's such a nice bird. He sleeps through the night. And he already knows how to fly. He's just so sweet."

"That's nice," she agreed. "What kind of a bird is he?"

How could I tell her?

I continued talking even faster. "He's no trouble at all. He loves everyone. And he smiles all the time!"

Then she interrupted me, "But what *kind* of a bird is he?"

Talking a mile a minute, I answered, "Well, he's a starling but he thinks he's an eagle because I've been telling him he's an eagle so he's got the heart of an eagle—"

"Wait!" she interrupted. "It's OK for him to be a starling. He doesn't have to be an eagle. We'll take him and love him whatever he is. It's OK for him to be a starling."

Friends, it's OK to be a starling. The world is full of starlings, and you know that I'm not talking about birds. I think probably many of us are starlings. And that includes me.

But it's OK to be a starling. God loves the starlings of the world. It's OK to be just what you are. God is not asking you be something you are not. You don't have to be an eagle or a hummingbird or a peacock. God loves *you*. That's why He chose you.

I love the encouraging words in James 1:18: "In his goodness he chose to make us his own children. . . . And we, out of all creation, became his choice possession" (NLT).

But why?

Why did God choose me?

Doesn't He remember my family history? Doesn't He remember that my father was an alcoholic? Doesn't He know that nearly every uncle on my father's side was an alcoholic, and almost every aunt was married to an alcoholic? Doesn't He know it's in my very genes, that it's part of my earliest memories?

Doesn't God see my struggles every day?

Doesn't He know how hard I try to be like Him and find myself failing too often?

Yes, God knows Ginny Allen's family history. And He knows your family history too. He knows my struggles and your struggles too. But still He chose you and He chose me.

But why, why did God choose me? And you? What difference did it make to Him? Why did He bother?

The answer is found in Romans 1:6, 7: "You are among those who have been called to belong to Jesus Christ, dear friends in Rome. God loves you dearly, and he has called you to be his very own people" (NLT).

You were chosen to be His very own. You were called to belong to Jesus because He loves you dearly!

I have to tell you in all honesty that I don't completely understand it, but I believe it. And you may not completely understand it, but you can believe it too!

Chapter 18

Promises

My story isn't over yet.

Although I was getting better every day, I was still nauseated and throwing up because of the powerful antibiotics I was still getting. I was still connected to IVs and couldn't go home until the IVs were removed. But the IVs could not be removed until I was able to eat and drink without throwing up. Finally, the doctor decided to try Zofran, a powerful antiemetic, to stop my nausea and vomiting. The first two times the nurse gave it to me, the medicine seemed to help. The third time they gave it, I felt a little funny. But I was so miserable I thought it was just one more thing to deal with, another symptom among many.

The fourth time, as the nurse was giving Zofran through my IV, I suddenly lost control of my left arm. It rose up and wobbled in the air. Dave wondered if I was having a seizure, but I didn't know what was happening. Then I began to fall apart emotionally, crying hysterically. That was the beginning of an eight-hour panic attack interspersed with several more small seizures. I couldn't stop talking and cried much of the time. My nephew, Dr. Tom, a psychologist, came and tried to calm me down. Nothing worked. My sister-in-law Cheryl was the hospital nursing supervisor that night, and she spent most of that afternoon and evening in my room, also trying to help calm me down. Again, nothing worked.

Things that are funny now were not funny then.

At one point Cheryl offered to order some applesauce and crackers for my husband who had missed supper because I wouldn't let him leave my side. I didn't feel safe unless I could see him. As soon as I heard her say "applesauce," I sat straight up in bed crying out, "You can't give him applesauce!" Continuing hysterically, I questioned, "Don't you know applesauce kills people?"

I and the rest of my family have always loved applesauce, so my dire announcement was a little surprising to everyone. Cheryl tried to reason with me. "Now, Ginny," she said, "how many people do you know who have died eating applesauce?"

I thought deeply for three or four seconds before I declared emphatically, "Well, how would you know? They're all dead. They can't tell you!" We laugh now, but no one was laughing then.

I felt like I was going to die and kept asking Dave what was wrong. I asked him over and over if I was having a stroke. Holding my hand and stroking my arm, he assured me that I would be all right. At that point, no one knew quite what had happened or what had caused the panic attack. Finally, I asked Dave to promise that if I had a massive stroke he would let me go. I didn't want any heroics. No lifesaving measures. He was reluctant, but finally made the promise so I would calm down. That promise was very important in the light of what happened later that evening.

His promise helped me settle down for a little while, but soon I told him I wanted him to make another promise.

"What?" he asked.

I wanted him to promise that if I died, he would not marry again right away.

He said, "WHAT?"

I explained seriously that if he married right away, then everyone would think he was just waiting for me to die so he could go find someone else to marry. I wouldn't quit crying until he promised that he wouldn't marry right away again. Again, his promise calmed me down a bit.

But soon I told him that I wanted him to make one more promise. By now he didn't want to hear any more requests about promises, but I was so upset that he finally asked very tentatively, "What?"

I told him that I wanted him to promise that when he got married again—and he must remember that it couldn't be right away—that he would not marry "you know who." And he knew who! He knew I was referring to his old high school girlfriend.

"I haven't seen her in more than forty years!" he protested.

"I know that!" I said tearfully. "But if you marry her, everyone will say you never forgot her and you were just waiting for me to die so you could go find her."

He promised.

We had been married almost forty years, and during that time no one could have been more faithful and loving than my husband has been. But my mind was far away and my thoughts were uncontrollable and strange.

> *"He will not let you stumble; the one who watches*
> *over you will not slumber. Indeed, he who watches*
> *over Israel never slumbers or sleeps.*
> *The Lord himself watches over you!"*
> (Psalm 121:3–5, NLT).

One of the best things about God is that is He consistent. The word *consistent* is a stand-alone word. No modifiers. You can't be a "little" consistent, nor can you be "more" consistent. You are either consistent or you are not consistent. God is consistent. His character never changes. So we can know that when we are confused, when our minds are not clear, when our hearts are doing strange things, God is still the same. In His watch-care, in His understanding, in His love—God is consistent. "I am the LORD, I do not change" (Malachi 3:6, NKJV).

When we need Him the most, God is consistent. No matter what happens, you can know that God is consistent.

I discovered the joys of being a grandparent when our little Ashley Rae was born a number of years ago. Right after Ashley was born, I bought a grandmother pin. It says "Grandma" and little charms that represent each grandchild are hung on a bar beneath the word. In the charm is the birthstone for each grandchild. Until Kennedy was born, there was just one charm on the pin, the charm representing Ashley.

I wore my Grandma pin often. One day, after Ashley was old enough to notice the pin, she asked me why I wore it so often. Actually, what she said was, "Mimi, why you wear this *again*?"

I explained that it was because the little girl charm represented her, and when I wear it I think of her. I told her I always wear it over my heart because that is where she is, in my heart, and that I love her more than I can possibly tell her. I told her that I will always love her no matter what. I wish you could have seen the big smile that covered her little face.

She would often climb on to my lap to touch the charm that represented her. Then she would smile at me because we both knew what it meant, that she was in my heart, and I will always love her no matter what.

One day I was wearing a blouse with a pocket and the little charm kept falling in the pocket where it couldn't be seen. Later, when Ashley came over, I noticed that she kept glancing at my blouse but I didn't think too much about it. Later, I must have moved in such a way that the charm fell out of the pocket.

Immediately, Ashley came over to me. Climbing onto the couch beside me and reaching up, she softly touched the little charm. Immense relief flooded her face as she exclaimed, "Oh, *there* I am!"

You have a God who holds you in His heart and loves you so much no matter what. Even when you feel separated from Him, even when you cannot see exactly where you are with Him, you can be assured that you are in His heart. He is always thinking of you. Because He loves you no matter what. Perhaps He is waiting for you to discover where you are, to hear you say, "Oh, *there* I am!" Right there in His heart.

Thank You, God, for being consistent. In our lives and in Your love!

If you want a clear picture of God's no-matter-what love, spend some time reading the Bible. It is, after all, His love letter to you.

You will find the Bible is the story of a God who loves you so much that He invites, He begs, He explains, He advises, He cajoles, He entreats, He pleads, He romances, He calls, He shouts, He whispers, He cries—to convince you of His love. All of these He does so you will choose to love Him back. You see, that is the great unknown in the Bible. That's the question that Scripture can't answer because it hasn't been written yet. Who will you choose to love? If the Bible were being written today, if your story was included as part of Scripture, what would it tell of your choice?

By the way, God wants you not just to love Him but to like being with Him better than anyone else in the whole world. He wants you to know Him and love Him and understand Him, heart and soul. God wants His love story with you to never end.

It's interesting that most of the love songs written today are about broken love relationships, unfaithfulness, cheating, and moving on. The emphasis, unfortunately, is usually on failed love stories. Lost love. But God's emphasis is always on His never-ending love. Again and again when Scripture talks about God's love, the Bible uses words such as *enduring, unfailing, eternal, abounding.*

Here are just a few of the many, many verses that tell you how God loves you:

First Chronicles 16:34 tells us that "his love endures forever." This phrase is used again and again. In fact, it is found forty-one times in the Old Testament, mostly in the book of Psalms. "His love endures forever"—a good fact, and a promise to hold in your heart.

Quickly read the following promises to get the scope of God's love for His people. Then go back and read them slowly, putting your name in each verse to get the impact of God's personal love for you.

"The earth is full of his unfailing love" (Psalm 33:5).

"How priceless is your unfailing love!" (Psalm 36:7).

"Great is your love, reaching to the heavens; your faithfulness reaches to the skies" (Psalm 57:10).

"Show us your unfailing love" (Psalm 85:7).

"You . . . are . . . abounding in love" (Psalm 86:5).

"Great is your love toward me" (Psalm 86:13).

"As high as the heavens are above the earth, so great is his love for those who fear him" (Psalm 103:11).

"From everlasting to everlasting the LORD's love is with those who fear him" (Psalm 103:17).

"Save me according to your unfailing love" (Psalm 109:26).

"Though the mountains be shaken and the hills be removed, yet my unfailing love for you will not be shaken" (Isaiah 54:10).

"You are precious to me and honored, and I love you" (Isaiah 43:4, TLB).

Can you even begin to imagine that God, the eternal, immortal God of all creation, calls *you* "honored"? Not only are you precious to Him, but you are honored!

I encourage you to read the Bible through at least once in your life. That is the only way that you will get a complete picture of God. It is a picture of a God who loves you so much that He will do whatever it takes to save you. In the Bible, we see a God who sometimes had to carry His children. Other times, He had to scold His children. And sometimes, the only way that God could get the attention of His children was to shout and scold and even spank them. But no matter what, He always loved His children.

Read your Bible as God's love letter to you, looking for all the ways He loves you. Underline those verses. Put your name in them. They are for you.

When my children come over and we're not home, they often leave little notes on the kitchen counter just so we know they stopped by, so we know they were there. Those little notes wouldn't matter to anyone else in the world, but they're priceless to me. Even when they say things like, "Just stopped by to use the bathroom," or, "I was hungry so I ate." They are usually signed "Love you!"

I am always sorry I missed seeing them.

When I see those little notes on the counter, it says to me that my son and daughters-in-law know that this is still their home, and they can come in anytime. It says they know they are welcome and loved, and looked for and wanted. The unwritten message of those notes tells me that they wish I'd been home.

Your time with God is precious to Him. He wants you to know you are welcome and loved and looked for and wanted. When you don't spend time with Him, He misses you. It leaves a hole in His heart that nothing else can fill.

So I encourage you to read His notes to you.

Thank You once again, Lord, for being consistent.

Thank You for being consistent in our lives and in Your love.

Chapter 19

From Bad to Worse

After eight hours in a panic attack, I was exhausted. My symptoms gradually lessened, and I finally fell into a deep sleep. And all the family members who had gathered in my room thought the ordeal was over and went home. They assumed the medicine was out of my system.

Everyone went home, that is, but my husband. Every night for the three weeks I had been in the hospital, Dave slept in a chair beside my bed. He had also spent his days sitting with me, only occasionally going to his brother's home to freshen up. This night he, too, was exhausted, and as he usually did, he fell asleep in his chair while holding my hand.

He had only been sleeping for about forty minutes when he was awakened as I jerked my hand out of his. He looked over and realized that I was having a grand mal seizure. He quickly checked my breathing and pulse. No breathing. No pulse. My heart had stopped.

Terrified, he ran out to the nurses' station calling, "My wife has coded! She's not breathing!"

Instantly, the room filled with nurses dragging the crash cart and then doctors hurrying to resuscitate me. Cheryl arrived again and led Dave out of the room to the end of the hall where he could wait in a small empty room. He was stunned. He had just buried his son and now, almost six months to the day, his wife might also be dead. Later he said that was the longest ten-minute wait of his life. He asked God over and over, "God, how can I go home without my wife!"

Finally, Cheryl came in to tell him, "We got her back."

The next thirty-six hours my husband never left my side in the intensive care unit. Though he was tired and now it was after midnight, he stood by my bed and watched the screen monitoring my vital signs as many hours later my racing heart finally started to slow down.

The doctor had initially exclaimed, "It can't be the Zofran!" He went to a computer and to his books to research everything he could find on this medicine. Coming back with an open book in his hand, he said, "It *was* the Zofran."

Zofran is the answer for most people who suffer with uncontrollable nausea and vomiting, especially cancer patients. He explained that very few people have a reaction to Zofran. And later, he told me that it is very rare to have a panic attack with Zofran. It is even more rare to have a grand mal seizure. And it is most rare of all to go into anaphylactic shock, or code, when using Zofran. Then my doctor said, "You did all three in the space of eight hours! If you ever take Zofran again, you won't live to tell the story."

About a week later, nineteen days after I had been admitted, I was released from the hospital. I flew home the next day. I was weak but alive. The kidney that doctors thought would never heal was healing. I truly owe my life and my healing to God. I am loved.

I can never thank my faithful husband enough for his watch-care over me. Had he not been sleeping by my bed and holding my hand, I would not be here to tell the story. Once again, I am loved.

> *"I have loved you, my people, with an everlasting love.*
> *With unfailing love I have drawn you to myself"*
> (Jeremiah 31:3, NLT).

I recognize that every day I live is a special gift. It could so easily have ended differently. Death is painful beyond words for those left to mourn, perhaps because death was never meant to be. It was not in God's original plan for His newly created children. They were meant to live forever.

For many years I was the school nurse at Auburn Academy, which is a boarding high school near Seattle, Washington. Early one morning, I was seeing sick girls in the clinic in the girls' dorm when suddenly a girl burst into the room. She said just two words. "He's dead."

Everybody in the room turned and looked at her. We were stunned. Then she turned around and ran from the room. Sometimes the students would get an early morning or late night phone call telling them of the death of a relative. I assumed that she had received such a call. So I wondered who had died.

I went out to find her. She was sitting on the floor in the hall just outside the clinic, her back against the wall, and her face buried in her hands. She was sobbing uncontrollably.

I sat down beside her and began to question her, "Janice, honey, what happened?"

"I don't know!" she sobbed. "He's just dead!"

"Who is it, dear? Who died?"

She sobbed harder. But finally she got it out. "Nicki!" she cried. "Nicki is dead."

Now I knew her family and couldn't think of anyone named Nicki. So I asked, "How did you find out? Did someone call you?"

Tears streaming, she said, "I went to take a shower, and when I came back to my room I found him dead."

Now this was the girls' dorm at six-thirty in the morning, so now I couldn't help wondering, Who was the "he" she found dead in her room?

"Well, Janice," I asked, "who is Nicki?"

At that, she sobbed even harder, but finally she was able to reply. "Nicki," she said, "is the hamster that Greg gave me for Valentine's Day."

Oh, no, I thought. *All this for a dumb dead hamster!*

See, I don't know about you, but I had been the hamster route. I well remember the day my two little boys brought home two hamsters with the assurances that they were both the same sex. And let me tell you, you don't know that for sure until they either have babies or they don't have babies, for there is no such thing as an infertile hamster. Soon we had babies coming out our ears. We gave the daddy away.

Now I have always loved animals, but I soon discovered I didn't care much for hamsters. It was a little upsetting when they kept escaping from the expensive escape-proof Habitrail bought especially for their comfort and enjoyment. It was more upsetting when one of them lived in the piano for several days, and I could hear him chewing on the felt pads.

But it was most upsetting when I found that some hamster moms have no qualms about eating their babies. As day after day I saw the number of babies decrease, I discovered that I really didn't care for hamsters. Then came the day I found the mom eating her adolescent son, the last of the litter, who was nearly as big as she was! So I knew very clearly how I felt about hamsters.

So you can see why I wasn't particularly moved by Nicki's problem. But I was moved by how Janice felt about Nicki's problem. Sighing, I said to her, "Well, let's go have a look at him."

On the way to her room, she explained that he had gotten caught under his exercise wheel, he wasn't breathing, and his lips were blue. We walked into her room, and I saw that she was right. Nicki wasn't breathing and his lips really were blue. There was no heartbeat. He was definitely dead.

As I stood there looking down on Nicki, I was thinking that the only good hamster might be a dead hamster, but there stood Janice sobbing beside me. So I knew what I had to do.

Have you ever done CPR on a dead hamster?

Now prior to this, I had done mouth-to-beak on a blue jay and it had lived, but with this hamster, there was no telling where his lips had been. But I began massaging his little chest and blowing into his little blue muzzle. Again and again I kept pumping his limbs and massaging his heart and blowing into his little blue lips. I continued this for probably five or six minutes.

Then all of a sudden, Nicki shuddered all over, gasped, and took a deep breath. He opened his eyes, and if he could have talked, I know he would have said, "Where am I?"

Well, he lived although he did have a little bit of brain damage from lack of oxygen. After his near-death experience, he always leaned a bit to the left as he walked.

Of course, this was written up in the Auburn school newspaper on the front page with banner headlines, SCHOOL NURSE SAVES LIFE! But it wasn't until the last line that the story mentioned Nicki was a hamster. Well, you can imagine the comments that people made for months because this newspaper was sent out to parents of our students all over the state. For one thing, they kept asking if my husband still kissed me.

They would ask me, "Do you know what hamsters do?"

Did *I* know? If anyone knew exactly what hamsters do, wasn't it me? But mostly what I heard again and again was, "Ginny, why did you bother?" "Why did you bother with that dumb little hamster? It was only a hamster!" "Hamsters are a dime a dozen! You could have gone to any pet store and bought another one. There are plenty more of them. Why did you bother?"

I often wonder if the angels ever asked God, "Why do You bother with those people? Do You know what they do? God, You could begin again and create a whole new world! Why do You bother? These people go places they shouldn't go. They listen to things they shouldn't listen to. They eat things they shouldn't eat."

This disobedience began in the Garden of Eden. It quickly grew to the point that the Bible says that God "saw the wickedness of man . . . , and He was grieved in His heart" (Genesis 6:5, 6, NKJV). He was sorry in His heart that He had made humans.

And King David must have been so unhappy and disgusted with those around him that he wrote to God, "I cannot understand how you can bother with mere puny man" (Psalm 8:3, TLB).

But it gets worse. Are you aware that Psalm 106:37 tells us that parents even sacrificed their own sons and daughters? These were God's chosen people doing that terrible thing, following the religious customs of their pagan neighbors. God said, rather desperately, that He "never commanded, nor did it enter my mind, that they should do such a detestable thing" (Jeremiah 32:35; see also verses 33 and 34).

But just a few verses beyond that statement, God says, "I will bring them back . . . and let them live in safety. They will be my people" (Jeremiah 33:37, 38). As long as there is a spark of hope for our salvation, God does not give up.

I think the angels must have even wondered if the plan of salvation had been wasted on mankind who didn't seem to appreciate the gift!

But I want to tell you that the good news today is that God knows exactly what you are! God knows exactly what you do! And yet this is what He is saying to you and to me, "I have created you and cared for you since you were born. I will be your God through all your lifetime, yes, even when your hair is white with age. I made you and I will care for you. I will carry you along and be your Savior" (Isaiah 46:3, 4, TLB).

Listen to God speaking in Isaiah 44:21, 22: "I made you, and I will not forget to help you. I have blotted out your sins; they are gone like morning mist at noon!" (TLB). He says in Isaiah 43:4—and He's talking to *you*—"You are precious to me and honored, and I love you" (TLB). Be sure to see how important this is. Many places in the Bible *tell* you that God loves you, but in this passage the words are spoken by God Himself.

I think that probably after the Cross, the angels never asked that question again because they saw the value that God places on His earthly children. They saw what people were worth to God. They saw the price that was paid for you.

Chapter 20

No Untouchables

My husband and I love spreading the good news of God's love both here in the United States and in other countries. In the summer of 2001, we were in Mwanza, Tanzania, working with the Africa for Christ evangelistic meetings. Our schedule was busy; we had off just one day a week to relax and catch up on things. One of those Thursdays, our whole group went for a boat ride on Lake Victoria. Now that may sound pretty nice, but I want to remind you that you didn't see the boat! It was an inter-island mail boat that also acted as the local ferry.

During one of the tiny island stops, we had about an hour to walk around. The captain took us to a few cages that housed some animals. One of those cages held a big, beautiful, black, hairy chimp. We were told we could feed him and that he liked anything and everything. People started rummaging through bags and purses looking for something to give him. The chimp had a feast eating chips and candy and drinking pop and juice from bottles and cans.

Standing wistfully by, I wished I, too, had something to feed him. A friend nearby said, "Ginny, I think I have an apple in my bag. Maybe we can split it and each of us give him half."

Of course, I was elated. My husband split the apple, and I trotted right up to the cage, stretching my arm toward him, the apple lying on my palm. The chimp looked at the apple and then looked at me. With one hand he reached out and took the apple. With his other hand he grabbed hold of my now empty hand. Meanwhile, his eyes never left mine.

He ate the apple while holding on to my hand. When he finished eating, he used both of his hands, one continued to hold tightly to my hand and the other softly, gently stroked my arm over and over. Gazing lovingly into my eyes, he kept on stroking and caressing my arm for at least ten minutes.

Finally, my husband, who had been watching all this, approached the cage and told the big, black, beautiful chimp, "Don't get any ideas, buddy. She's taken!"

My friend quickly brought her apple to Mr. Chimp, but he simply took the apple and ignored her. In fact, he ignored everyone else too, although he happily took the food they offered.

It was only me whose hands he held and stroked and caressed. His owner said to me, "He likes you. He has chosen only you."

There's something special about being chosen. Even when it is just a big old chimp doing the choosing! Every time I remember that big old hairy hand holding mine, gently rubbing my arm, I am enthralled all over again. It is a magical moment for me.

There's something very special about being chosen.

And you and I are chosen. The apostle Paul reminds us. "We know, dear brothers and sisters, that God loves you and has chosen you to be his own people" (1 Thessalonians 1:4, NLT). We are chosen by the King of kings, the Lord of lords. We are chosen by Jesus, our Savior, our Redeemer, our Brother, our best Friend, the great Lover of our souls. Never forget for a moment that you are chosen.

"You didn't choose me. I chose you"
(John 15:16, NLT).

Fast-forward nine years to August 2010. We were again in Africa, this time in Kisii, Kenya. We were once again helping with evangelistic meetings.

One evening, I had finished my talk on health and sat down in a chair behind the speaking platform but still in the podium area. I had just put down my computer and settled onto the hard wooden chair, when a movement to the side of the platform caught my attention. I looked over to find the dirtiest, most raggedy looking human being I have ever seen coming toward me.

Now I want you to know that I have seen poverty too many times in my life not to recognize it. I have been on many mission trips to Mexico and have driven through the squalor of the border towns. I have visited the favelas in São Paulo, Brazil—considered to be some of the worst slums in the world. I have seen the shanties in Cape Town and Johannesburg in South Africa. A few years ago, we spent a few days in Calcutta, where we saw the "poorest of the poor," as Mother Teresa called them, sleeping on the streets and in the gutters. So I am well familiar with poverty and dirt.

But this man was the worst of everything I have ever seen. His clothes, his body, his face, and his hands were caked with grime, dirt literally worn into them and hanging from them. And as he walked toward me, he was smiling and holding out his hands.

Most of my friends and acquaintances know that I love animals and children. But even those who know me very well probably don't know this one thing about me. I like for my hands to be clean. I'm not fanatic or compulsive. I just like clean hands. I don't particularly like to garden because I don't like the dirt under my fingernails. I don't like to make bread because I hate the feeling of the dough gummed up on my hands. You get the picture.

Now here was this man, this ragged, filthy man, holding out his hands to me. All of this happened much more quickly than I can tell it. It was just a matter of seconds. My heart almost stopped as I realized what was happening. But I am glad that my response was just what it should have been.

Without missing a beat, I caught his dirty hands with my own clean hand. He took my hand in both of his and then I reached forward and covered his hands with my other clean hand. I barely had time to wonder where those hands had been, to wonder how long it had been since soap and water had been a part of his life. He talked to me in Swahili for a few minutes, smiling vacantly and caressing my hands the whole time. Then he turned and wandered back to his seat, where he continued to watch me.

I wanted to wash my hands! I *needed* to wash my hands! And I had hand sanitizer in my pocket. But I knew instinctively that I couldn't use it. What kind of message would that have given him?

So I just sat there trying not to touch anything and trying not to look at him. But I couldn't help myself. Every time I glanced over toward him, he would get up and come to me with hands outstretched. We went through this process three or four times, and then a deacon saw what was happening and escorted him from behind the podium to a place in the audience where he couldn't reach me.

Isn't it interesting that I was so thrilled when a chimp held my hand, and never once did I question where *his* leathery hands had been! Have you ever watched, really watched, a chimp? Have you seen what they do with their hands? They pick their noses, and a few other things, quite happily! Yet I didn't wonder or question. I was simply thrilled with the moment.

But with this man, this fellow human being—my heart stood still with unspoken questions.

Later that night when we got back to our room, I told my husband about it. I had a hard time going to sleep. I couldn't stop thinking about what had happened. I woke up several times in the night going over it again and again in my mind. I was glad that though my heart had hesitated, my hands had not. I had done what needed to be done.

In the early morning hours after the long, restless night, finally it came to me. It was one of those moments that you know God has spoken to you, and this is what I heard. For Jesus there were no "untouchables." His heart did not hesitate as His hands reached out to those who needed to be touched. To walk through the Gospels is to see a Savior who did not know the word *untouchable.*

No one was too ugly or dirty or diseased or wretched or hopeless or sinful for Jesus to touch. For Jesus there were no untouchables. Blind beggars. Loathsome lepers. Noisy, sweaty, boisterous children. An enemy who needed his bloody ear reattached. Even the bier of a dead boy knew the touch of His life-giving hand.

Has Jesus touched your life? Have you let Him look at not just the best in you but at the worst in you? Have you let Him touch those areas that you would rather no one saw or even knew about? Remember that the word *untouchable* is not in the vocabulary of Jesus. Also remember that there is nothing you can tell Him that will surprise Him. He knows more about you than you know about yourself. And, in spite of what you are, or are not, He loves you.

There is nothing you can do that will make Him love you less, and there is nothing you can do that will make Him love you more. His love for you is not based on what you do or what you don't do. He loves you. Period. The promise in 1 John 3:1 is meant to encourage us: "See how much the Father has loved us! His love is so great that we are called God's children—and so, in fact, we are" (TEV).

What you do or don't do may make Him happy or unhappy, but it does not change His love for you. His love is eternal and unchangeable and personal. The good news is that He loves you too much to leave you the way you are. That's why He wants to touch your life. He's reaching out. Move a little closer so He can touch your heart.

Chapter 21

Free Wash

As I think of God's great love for me, I am determined to let Him make me into exactly what He wants me to be. This means I let Him decide what stays and what goes in my life.

One day I had just filled my car with gas when my eye fell on the sign, "Free car wash with a fill-up." My husband usually washes my car, but I decided to surprise him by saving him a little work on this Friday afternoon. I pulled around to the car wash, rolled my window down, and put the token into the slot. Then, after reading the instructions, I pulled forward to where the machine grabs onto the car. I put it in park and waited.

I am always fascinated by those giant brushes that twirl and swirl and swab and scrub with no effort on my part. So I was sort of scrunched forward watching the approach of blue bristles that were at least a foot-and-a-half long. The brushes hit the windshield along with a torrent of water, and in the next moment, I received the worst face-washing of my life. The big blue brushes along the side reached in and pounded my cheek, swabbing out my ear clear down to the drum. Of course, I had no idea what was happening, so I turned to look—just in time for the second set of brushes to complete the job!

Yes, I finally got the window rolled up. And as I peered out through the soapsuds running down from my eyebrows, I vowed I would tell no one about this super-shower situation. But, of course, I went straight home and told my husband in great detail how it felt to be scrubbed squeaky clean. He was just glad the whole thing was free.

God tells us, "Wash yourselves and make yourselves clean" (Isaiah 1:16, ERV). And again, He says, "O, Jerusalem, wash your heart from wickedness, that you may be saved" (Jeremiah 4:14, NKJV). I don't know how it is with you, but I struggle to be like Jesus. My heart is willing but my habits hang on. I'd like to be scrubbed up and squeaky clean spiritually.

But when I wash myself, I'm pretty gentle. I don't seem to do what needs to be done. I understand why David asked God to do the job for him, begging God to "wash me thoroughly from my iniquity, and cleanse me from my sin" (Psalm 51:2, NKJV). And verse 7 continues, "Wash me, and I shall be whiter than snow."

I am thankful, too, that God is gentle when I give Him permission to clean me up, to do what needs to be done in my life. And His help is free. No tokens needed.

> *"Wash me thoroughly from my iniquity,*
> *and cleanse me from my sin. . . .*
> *Wash me, and I shall be whiter than snow"*
> (Psalm 51:2–7, NKJV).

I am also thankful that God recognizes when I need His cleansing power, and He does not hesitate to help me out. No matter how dirty I am!

I was speaking for a pastors' wives' retreat in central California. After the morning meeting, we headed to lunch at the Soquel campgrounds dining hall. It was a beautiful day with blue skies and warm sunny breezes. It had rained the night before, and there were a few little puddles along the way. As we walked, I saw off to the side a large mud slick. It was about four feet by six feet with a surface that was satin smooth.

After lunch, I left the others and walked alone back to the lodge so I could study my notes for the next meeting. I don't even know what I was thinking about, but all of a sudden, I saw it again. The mud slick. In that instant, I knew immediately what I had to do. I had to make footprints in the mud.

Let me explain. I am one of those people who love to make footprints in untracked snow. I grew up in the Midwest, and I have wonderful memories of making tracks through deep, fresh snow. Now I live in the Pacific Northwest, and I love to make footprints in unmarked sand at the beach. At the ocean the waves are always leaving a clean palette for my feet. Now right here in front of me was a large expanse of slick, smooth mud, shiny and inviting.

Now I want you to know that I didn't make a conscious decision. I certainly didn't weigh the consequences. I really didn't think about it at all. In my heart, I just knew that I had to make footprints in that smooth, shiny mud. So, changing my course, I walked deliberately into the mud.

A heartbeat later, I lay flat on my back in that smooth, shiny mud!

At first I couldn't quite comprehend what had happened, but then came the realization that I was lying right smack in the middle of the mud slick. Even my head was in the mud. I could feel the wet mud in my hair. I was wearing dress-up clothes, and I could imagine what they looked like now.

But as quickly as those thoughts came, they were crowded out by another, more urgent, impulse. *Get out of the mud! Quick! What will people think? They'll think you're crazy if they see you here in the mud. They'll wonder what in the world you were doing. Why would anyone deliberately walk in mud?*

I scrambled to get out of the mud but rapidly discovered what probably everyone else already knew. It's not easy to get out of slick mud. I couldn't stand up, and it was too far to the edge of the mud slick for me to reach out and get hold of the dry concrete. I ended up crawling on my hands and knees, slipping and sliding, until I finally reached the edge of the mud slick—and dry ground. When I was finally able to stand, I ran to my room, changed out of my muddy clothes, scrubbed the mud out of my hair and off my body, rinsed my clothes, and took a deep breath. No one had seen me. No one would ever know.

But as I stood there alone in my room, I began to laugh. Here I was trying to hide the fact that I had fallen in the mud when wet and dripping church clothes were hanging all over my room. And all I could think of was how embarrassed I felt.

I had an aching bump on the back of my head where it had hit the concrete, and here I was, concerned only about what people might think of me. Would they think I was crazy? Why would someone my age try to walk in mud? For that matter, why would anyone *want* to walk in mud?

Didn't I understand what might happen? Surely I knew how slippery mud could be! And, of course, at the very next meeting, I had to tell the whole story because by now it struck me as very funny indeed.

The women checked the bump on my head, and they clucked in sympathy. And, of course, they laughed with me. But not one of them said, "Why in the world did you do something so dumb?" No one scolded, "Didn't you know what would happen?" No one even muttered, "I would have thought you were smarter than that!"

Instead, they all said things like, "You should have called for help!" "I would have helped you." "I'm sorry you got hurt." "Are you OK?"

One of my favorite Bible verses tells me, "God demonstrates His own love toward us, in that while we were yet sinners, Christ died for us" (Romans 5:8, NKJV). The little word *yet,* or as some translations say, *still,* is huge in this verse. "While we were still sinners . . . "

That little word tells me that God doesn't wait for us to crawl out of the mud and clean ourselves up. And He doesn't wait until we have washed away all the signs of mud and hung everything out to dry, hoping that no one will know, pretending that nothing has happened.

He comes to us while we are still in the mud, slipping and sliding, looking for the way out, grasping and clutching toward dry ground. And He picks us up out of the mud while He says to us, "I'm sorry you got hurt. Are you OK? I'm so glad you called Me. I'm always here to help you." Here's the promise: "I will strengthen you. I will help you" (Isaiah 41:10, NLT).

So here's the question. When you see someone who has fallen in the mud of life, what words come to your mind?

Have you ever heard someone say things like, "Didn't he know what would happen if he kept on drinking?" "How could she be so dumb?" "What goes around comes around!" "He made his bed; now he can lie in it." "It's not my problem."

It's easy to say those words when we pass by the unknown drunk wallowing in the mud of the gutter or the chain-smoking stranger with death-dealing carcinogens wafting about her head. After all, we have nothing invested in him or her, so we can make a clear judgment of the whole situation. Maybe it's easier to be tolerant of the mud when the person is someone we truly love. But then again, maybe not.

Sometimes we are hardest on those closest to us. The wayward son. The belligerent daughter. The obtuse spouse. Maybe too often we hear ourselves saying, "I tried to tell her. But would she listen? No!" Or, "He had to learn the hard way." Or even, "It's their own fault."

Maybe that's why the apostle Paul's advice is so important: "Let your gentleness be evident to all" (Philippians 4:5). And check out Hebrews 13:1: "Keep on loving each other as brothers."

Maybe we should ask God to give us His responses to these kinds of situations. "Are you OK?" "I would have helped you." "I'm sorry you got hurt."

And maybe, just maybe, we are hardest of all on ourselves.

We hear our own voice saying, "I just can't help it." Or, "It's no use. I'll never change!"

The day I fell in the mud, I could have gone to my room and simply changed my clothes. I could have put on long pants and long sleeves, brushed my hair, and gone on my way. No one would have known. It took more work and more time to wash away the mud, but it had to be done. Otherwise, I would have had to keep on hiding the mud, and then keep on, and keep on hiding the mud.

See, we can hide the fact that we've been in the mud, but hiding it doesn't change the fact that that's where we've been. Other people may not be able to see your mud, but God knows all about the mud slicks of your life, whether they show or not. Maybe that's why God encourages us to "wash yourselves and make yourselves clean" (Isaiah 1:16, ERV).

Of course, for some people, the mud slick becomes a way of life. They become comfortable there. It takes too much effort, too much work, to try to get out. So even though they slip and slide through life, it becomes easier to stay in the mud than to climb out onto dry ground. That's what the gospel message is all about. Jesus said He came to find those who are lost, to seek them out, and to save them from the mud slicks of life.

So what did I learn the day I tried to make mud prints?

First, that being in the mud is no place for a Christian. "God did not call us to be impure, but to live a holy life" (1 Thessalonians 4:7).

Second, that getting out of the mud is harder than you think. That's why God gives us these promises: "Call to Me, and I will answer you" (Jeremiah 33:3, NKJV), and "I will strengthen you and help you" (Isaiah 41:10, NLT).

Third, I learned that mud slicks look nicer than they really are. "Keep watch and pray that you will not fall into temptation" (Matthew 26:41, TEV). "There is a way that seems right to a man, but in the end it leads to death" (Proverbs 14:12).

Fourth, and most important, I learned that I can call for help when I need it without worrying about what other people will think. "I waited patiently for the LORD; he turned to me and heard my cry. He lifted me out of the slimy pit, out of the mud and mire; he set my feet on a rock and gave me a firm place to stand" (Psalm 40:1, 2).

Are you like me, wanting God to come into your heart and change your life?

He is just waiting for you to ask.

Anyway, I think I'll stick to making tracks in fresh snow. Or maybe sand prints along the beach. One thing I know for sure—no more mud slicks for me!

Blessed, So Very Blessed

I am blessed, so very blessed. Life is good and I am happy. I have a faithful husband who adores me. Soon we will celebrate fifty years together. They have been fifty happy years in spite of the great loss of our son, Bob. We cherish the memories of the thirty-five years we had him. One day shortly after the amazing fireman's funeral for our son, Dave said to me, "You know, we had him for thirty-five years, and it was not enough. But if we had had him for another thirty-five years, it would not have been enough. Only eternity will be enough when you love someone. And we have eternity coming!"

Scott and his wife, Cathie, live nearby, and we enjoy the many hours we spend with them. I could not imagine a better son. He gave us the gift of a daughter, not just a daughter-in-law, when he married his Cathie.

Then there is Dana, our second daughter-in-law. She is an amazing mother and a wonderful daughter-in-law. We could not love a daughter of our blood more than we love both of these women.

Our two granddaughters, Ashley and Kennedy, continue to bring unimaginable joy into our lives. They are sweet, caring, considerate girls who love God and try hard to live for Him.

In every story there are unanswered questions. People often ask, "What happened to your birth father?"

When he died in his eighties, he died with the hope of eternal life in his heart. He was a born-again Christian, a Lutheran lay pastor. What made the difference in his life? His wife, my stepmother Doris, never gave up on him. She must have seen something of value in him because for many years she continued to drag him home from bars and taverns. I do not know exactly what happened because I was not there. All I know is that her persistence brought him to Jesus, and his life was changed forever. He never drank alcohol again, and he gave his life to serving God.

So why have I told you my story? I have not told you my story to make you cry—and certainly not to make you feel sorry for me. I have told you my story to give you hope.

I want you to know that I recognize that my story is no different from many of yours. In fact, many of you have suffered far more than I have. I also recognize that there are things that are worse than death. Much worse. And some of you have gone through, or are going through, those things right now.

So first, I believe that you and I need to show the world that a relationship with Jesus makes a difference, no matter what is happening in our lives. But we can know that only if we have been spending time with Him, if we have that relationship with Him.

There are people who lose their child, and they lose their faith. There are people who lose their spouse, and they lose their trust. Of course, we hurt and we cry and we sorrow like everyone else does, but I love what God says in 1 Thessalonians 4:13. It doesn't say you won't grieve, but it says your sorrow will not be like the sorrow of those who have no hope.

Because it is so important, I want to say it again.

Our lives are to show the world that no matter what is happening in our lives, it makes a difference to be in a relationship with Jesus.

And second, I am telling my story to encourage you to hang on. No matter how hard life is, no matter what decisions others around you are making—and that includes the people you love most—hang on to Jesus. It's not enough to know God in the sunshine. We have to know Him in the shadows. We have to know Him when the night is so black we can't even breathe. We have to know Him when our world collapses around us, and there are no answers to our questions. When our hearts are ripped apart with pain, we have to know who is holding our hand. We have to know God's heart. A heart that says, "I am the LORD your God. I am holding your hand, so don't be afraid. I am here to help" (Isaiah 41:13, CEV).

> *"As for me, I know that my Redeemer lives,*
> *and that he will stand upon the earth at last.*
> *And after my body has decayed, yet in my body*
> *I will see God! I will see him for myself.*
> *Yes, I will see him with my own eyes.*
> *I am overwhelmed at the thought!"*
> (Job 19:25–27, NLT).

Since Chicago played such an important part of my life, I am a Cubs fan, although I actually find professional baseball a little slow. One time, when we were back in Indiana visiting relatives, we took our young boys to a Cubs game in Chicago. I don't remember who the Cubs were playing, but I can tell you that it was not very exciting. In fact, by the ninth inning, the score was four to zero, and Chicago was the zero.

It was a foregone conclusion the Cubs would lose. You could see the stands starting to empty. At the beginning of the ninth inning, even more people started leaving. Most assumed it was over for the Cubs.

The other team finished at bat and it was Chicago's turn. It was the last half of the last inning.

The first batter struck out.

The second batter struck out.

Now the third batter came up and the pitch was thrown. It was a strike. The second ball came sizzling across the plate and the umpire called, "Strike two!"

Two outs and two strikes. By now the crowd was streaming out, and the stadium was nearly empty. The game was over for the Cubs and everyone knew it.

Then came the third pitch. The batter swung the bat. We heard the solid sound of the bat hitting the ball. The ball popped high out into left field. Few spectators paid attention as the fielder ran into position, with glove held high. They already knew what was going to happen. The ball landed as expected right in that glove.

But what happened next was not expected. The ball bounced out of the glove and rolled across the ball field. By the time the player recaptured it, the batter was safely on first base.

You see, the batter had taken off running the instant his bat hit the ball. He knew it wasn't over 'til it's over, so he ran. Now he found himself on first base and the crowd roared.

The next batter came to the plate. He had a base hit. Now there were two runners on base. The crowd again roared their approval. Batter number three filled the bases, and the relatively few Cubs fans left in the stadium filled the air with their shouts of encouragement.

Now batter number four crouched in position, bat in hand. It seemed that everyone in the stadium held their breath.

The pitcher wound up and threw the ball.

The batter swung hard—and hit a home run. And the Cubs went on to win the game. It was an incredible ending!

I was there. I saw it.

Newscasters later described what was happening outside the stadium, while the Cubs were winning inside the stadium. They said that as the first roar came up from the spectators, the people streaming through the gates stopped in their tracks.

With the second shouts resounding through the air, people began to run back to the stadium. Those still inside ran to where they could watch. Those outside the gates tried frantically to get in, but they couldn't. The gates had locked behind them. The people in their cars pulled over, glued to their radios.

And all of them wished, oh, how they wished, that they were inside those walls watching the victory. But they had counted their team out. They figured the game was over. But it wasn't over yet!

The Cubs won that day. An amazing victory!

My friend, the game of life is not over yet. Sometimes it may seem that our team—the team for God and all that is good—is losing. And the critical question for you and for me is simply this, Whose side are you on? Which team are you supporting? Will you stay by until the very end when victory is declared?

When the Cubs won, we were overjoyed. Overjoyed, but surprised. Very, very surprised.

In the game of life, we already know how it's going to end. We know which team will be victorious. Revelation 20:9 tells us what happens in the end to those who follow Satan: "Fire came down from heaven and destroyed Satan's army" (ERV).

That's the sad news.

But the good news, the great news, is found in the next chapter of Revelation, chapter 21:7: "All who win the victory will be given these blessings. I will be their God, and they will be my people" (CEV).

In the game of life, both you and I choose which team we will join.

When the shouts of joy go up, where will you be? Will you be outside the walls of the Holy City wishing you were inside, or will you be part of the joyous and eternal celebration inside? It's not over yet, folks, but it won't be long now. The Bible ends with one last promise. You'll find it in the next to the last verse in the Bible—Revelation 22:20. Jesus promises, "Surely I am coming quickly" (NKJV).

A number of years ago, I was thinking about heaven. This is what I wrote in my Bible that day: "If God had everyone in heaven but me, it would not be enough for Him. He wants me there, too, and He can't be happy unless I am there."

My dear Reader Friend, if God had everyone in heaven but *you,* it would not be enough for Him. He wants *you* there too. He can't be fully happy unless you are there.

Meet me there.

I'll be looking for you!

HOPE for NEPAL
WOMEN

Advocating Women's Health

More than 600,000 women in Nepal suffer from uterine prolapse and up to 200,000 of these need immediate surgery. Asian Aid has been active in providing women's health care and education in Nepal, sponsoring more than 10,000 life-changing surgeries.

Rescuing Women from Slavery

Since August 2010 Asian Aid has been sponsoring a highly successful team of 20 volunteers and a safe house in their efforts to rescue young Nepalese girls from human trafficking.

www.HopeNepalWomen.org

Asian Aid is a fully supportive ministry of the Adventist Church that sponsors over 8,000 children and operates orphanages and special schools with the church in India, Nepal, and Bangladesh. **Asian Aid projects include the Nepal women's project and other village development work.**

To receive more information on this project or how to sponsor a needy child, contact Asian Aid:

Asian Aid USA PO Box 2258, Collegedale TN 37315
toll-free: **1-866-569-7933** email: **support@asianaid.org**

www.asianaid.org